Sticky

Memorable Lessons
From Ordinary Moments

Notes

Matt Eicheldinger

Andrews McMeel
PUBLISHING®

Other Books by Matt Eicheldinger

Matt Sprouts and the Curse of the Ten Broken Toes

Matt Sprouts and the Day Nora Ate the Sun

For my students and the stories we share together.

Introduction

At their core, stories are used as a way for individuals to get to know each other, and we all have stories worth telling. However, sometimes the stories we capture, whether on purpose or by default, tend to miss the most extraordinary lessons, even from the simplest of situations.

I discovered this by accident.

When I started teaching sixth grade in 2009, one of my mentors told me I should write down a reflection after every lesson I taught so I could make adjustments the following year. Professionally, it would be in good practice to do so, even if it added time to my already crammed teaching schedule.

So I tried. I really did.

But it only lasted a couple of weeks. It felt like homework, and I didn't feel like I was gaining anything meaningful from it.

However, I did replace it with something else.

That same week, one of my students said something so unexpectedly funny I never wanted to forget it, so I wrote it down. Just a short, quick sentence with enough detail for me to remember the scene if I looked back on it years later. That's how it all started.

For the next fifteen years, I wrote down everything I wanted to remember from my sixth-grade classroom. I jotted things down in notebooks, electronic files, on gifts from students, more notebooks, and even next to their faces in yearbooks. For the most part, the memories just sat in those places, untouched for years.

But then, in the summer of 2023, I began going through all of those captured moments in time.

I expected to find exactly what I wrote down—a funny quote here, a story of friendship there, but instead, I discovered something more. There, in all those memories, were lessons.

I am not sure why I missed these in the moment, but now it is all I can see. Life lessons, embedded in the simplicity of everyday encounters, just waiting to be discovered. And what I know is this:

Everyone has a story to tell, and every story is important.

Every. Single. One.

The following stories took place in my sixth-grade classroom. The names of individuals have been changed for privacy.

However, one name has not been changed:

Tapasvi.

You will understand why when you read her story.

A Sticky Note

Years ago, I had a student who wouldn't speak.

And when I say "wouldn't speak,"

I mean, not at all.

Not one word.

I have never felt so ill-equipped as a teacher.

I had no tools for this situation.

So, as a way to help connect with her, I just drew a cartoon or wrote

a little message on a sticky note and placed it on her desk

every

single

day.

It went on like this for the rest of the year.

We had parent meetings,

counselor meetings,

psychologist meetings,

and we kept trying to talk to her,

but she didn't speak

all year.

Two years go by,

and I get an envelope in the mail.

What's inside?

A single sticky note.

On it, it said,

"I saved all your sticky notes. Thank you so much, you helped me more

than you know."

And that's what is hard about life.

Most of the time, you never get to know your impact.

But I guarantee you, whatever you are doing

even the small things

like a sticky note

have probably made a huge difference.

An Empty Chair

I had a student named Maya who lost her youngest sister to cancer.

She took about two weeks off from school

to be with her family

and before she came back, she sent us an email.

"The last two weeks have been really hard for me,

so when I come back to school,

I just don't want to talk about it."

We wanted to show that we cared,

but we also wanted to honor her request, so we did.

We didn't talk about it.

About a month later,

we were independently reading in class

when Maya stood up and walked over to me.

She was on the teetering edge of crying.

She said, "That chair next to your desk, can I use it?"

I nodded my head, then placed the empty chair next to hers,

and it just sat there,

empty.

At the end of class, she brought the chair back and said,

"Can I use this chair tomorrow? It helped me feel better."

That's when I realized the chair wasn't as empty as I thought it was.

When I went into teaching

I knew in general what I was going to experience,

I just had no idea how much moments like this

would change me.

Lightning

One of my first challenges as a teacher was trying to help

a student named K.J.

Teachers joke that kids run on the walls.

Well,

K.J. actually could.

He was like lightning

hitting all areas of the room, starting little fires

all the time.

His parents were great, K.J. was great,

but still,

his impulsiveness interrupted the flow of class constantly.

It was draining.

But one day, K.J.'s lightning was different.

We were on an outdoor field trip,

and kids were struggling to finish a snowshoe hike through the snow.

Everyone was complaining.

"I can't do it, Mr. Eich. It's too hard!"

"When are we going to be done? My legs hurt!"

That's when K.J. stepped in.

He was everywhere,

encouraging every classmate with a genuine kindness and energy

I cannot replicate.

Sometimes, you'll work with someone and get so caught up in

what you are trying to do

you end up missing the traits that are going to make someone

truly special.

And for K.J., it was his lightning—

the ability to be everywhere, all at once,

but especially when people needed him the most.

Silly Bandz

My third year teaching sixth grade, I had a student named Rachel,

who was one of the nicest kids you'll ever meet.

She had Silly Bandz, those small animal-shaped rubber bands

up to her elbows most days,

and a giggle that would make you want to join in on the fun.

But those giggles came and went as Rachel bounced back and forth

between living with Dad,

then Mom,

then Uncle,

then Grandparents.

She often looked disheveled and was constantly losing things:

her Silly Bandz,

her books,

her backpack.

It was to the point where most days she came with nothing.

So I made a plan.

"Hey, Rachel, I made you a backpack you can keep at school. It's got everything you need, and I even put a few Silly Bandz in there. And it will be here for you every day."

Rachel dug into the backpack. "It's mine?!" she said. "And I can keep it here at home?!"

"Yeah, it's yours, but I think you meant keep it here at school," I corrected.

"Well, the classroom is my home," she replied. "I'm here more than any other place."

There are days at work where it feels like work. But there are other days when I swear I am within an extended family.

That's what I think about when I see Silly Bandz.

The classroom isn't just a classroom.

For some,

it's home.

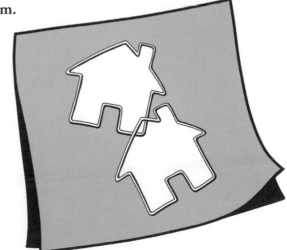

Minecraft

One of my students, Natasha, had a medical procedure that

required her to stay in the hospital for a month.

I checked in with her parents a few days after the procedure.

They said she really missed her friends at school,

so the class and I developed a plan.

During lunch each day,

a small group of students would come into my room

and use my computer to play the video game *Minecraft* online

with Natasha.

It was an instant morale boost for Natasha and her classmates,

but that is not where this story ends.

Natasha was having so much fun,

she invited other kids at the hospital to play with her

and the rest of the class.

It became such a hit that students went home

and continued to play *Minecraft* with kids from the hospital

who they had met through Natasha.

As a teacher, sometimes you think of your class

as a finite environment,

because you're in the same room all day,

and it's like that for many of us.

The same place.

Every day.

It feels restrictive.

But we forget to realize that the confines of that place also have the ability

to expand.

So that's what I think about when I see *Minecraft*.

You can build whatever kind of physical classroom you want,

but given the opportunity,

kids will take what you made

and turn it into something even better

than you could have possibly imagined.

A Dance

One of my students, Noah, came into my room with his friends,

and he was over-the-top happy.

"Hey, Noah!" I said. "What's with all the excitement?"

Noah's head was basically through the ceiling.

"She said yes!" he boasted. "Mr. Eich, I am going to the dance

with Britta!"

I love seeing students so happy when things work out,

but I also know the lows can quickly follow

the highs in middle school.

A few days later, I overheard the daily morning gossip

in the hall.

Britta wasn't going with Noah anymore.

So when Noah showed up in my room during my prep time,

I had a feeling what we would be talking about,

but we didn't.

"Can I just be in here?" he said. "I don't want to talk."

I nodded, and Noah took a seat for the rest of my prep period.

When he stood up at the end though,

what he said stuck with me.

"Thanks for the help, Mr. Eich."

"You're welcome buddy," I said. "But I didn't really do anything."

"Well, thanks for just being here," he said while grabbing his things.

"It means a lot."

Heartbreak can be hard, especially when it's new.

When we witness this with friends, family, or students,

we often feel a drive to fix and solve,

but sometimes you don't have to do any of those things.

Sometimes you just have to be present.

That's all.

A Scar

My students were working in teams, and one of them, Miguel,

kept stretching awkwardly and massaging his arm.

He wasn't shy about it either.

This was definitely a planned,

purposeful action.

His table was ignoring him, but he kept doing it.

This time he put his arm further in front of their faces

as he moaned and groaned in obviously fake pain.

Another kid finally spoke up.

"Hey, what's that on your arm?" the classmate said.

That was the single prompt Miguel was waiting for.

"Oh, this here?!" Miguel said, pointing to his arm. "It's a scar I got

from crashing on my bike last summer and sometimes it hurts. . . ."

The table listened to Miguel's story and then went back to work.

A few minutes later, I heard it again:

the moaning and groaning.

Miguel was standing at another table

doing the same thing as before.

I pulled him aside. "Hey, I think that might be distracting others."

"Oh," he said, hanging his head low.

"But," I continued. "Would you like to tell your story to *everyone* at the end of class?

Miguel almost exploded with excitement.

"Really?!" he asked. "That would be great!"

As a teacher, you work to build your classroom in a way where every student recognizes the importance of each other, because that's what you want for them in the world: a chance to be seen, heard, and understood.

A Pen

I had a student named Asher who had a problem with lying.

Like, he lied about *everything*.

He loved repeating one lie in particular about his pens.

"I have one million pens!" he said. "Seriously! No wait! It's actually TWO million!"

Students called him out on it all the time,

but that did not deter Asher from lying.

Unfortunately, his lying was so off-putting that no one really wanted to hang out with him.

One day, I had Asher eat lunch in my room,

and I asked him a question.

"Asher, what's your goal?"

"Huh?" he responded, confused.

"I know you lie, kind of often, like with the million pens," I pointed out. "So what's the goal? Why lie?"

He paused for a second and then said,

"I want to get more friends."

"I understand," I responded. "Well, is your plan

of lying working right now?"

He shook his head.

I think we all get trapped in repeating a plan

that doesn't work sometimes.

But for kids, some of them are stuck

because they don't know any other way,

so they just root down in the only plan they know.

Asher and I came up with a secret plan that day though.

We balanced a pen just above the board

at the front of the room

as a reminder of his pen lie.

And we spent many more lunches talking about other ways

to make friends.

So that's what I think about when I see pens.

People aren't stuck because they want to be.

They just need someone to teach them a new approach.

Folded Paper

We had a student, Kameel, join us midyear from a different country.

He had a bright smile,

was always eager to participate,

and made friends really quickly.

I noticed that every time he talked,

he always rubbed his necklace.

It was a greenish, thick square about an inch wide

and hung on a leather string.

You could tell it was really worn or used.

One day, I asked him if he would be willing to tell me a little more about his necklace.

He said, "It is folded paper, a ta'wiz. Prayers my family wrote for me.

Prayers for peace, love, and kindness, all folded up and bound together."

He paused, then continued.

"I rub it when I talk to people

because I know not everyone has those things,

so I send my family's prayers on to them."

As a teacher, I am lucky to be a witness to the good that lives in humanity.

Just unprompted extensions of love that trickle in when you least expect it

and it captures you in a way

you can't explain.

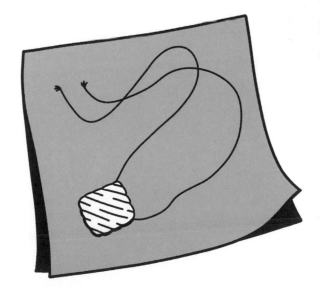

Perception

It was the first day of school. One of my students, Amir, was

quickly becoming a class favorite.

His energy was infectious.

He had kids laughing.

Everyone wanted to be his partner,

and I noticed he was especially good at one thing:

avoiding work.

For weeks, he did absolutely nothing.

Nothing.

His parents never returned a phone call or an email,

so it was just me

and Amir.

But the more I learned about Amir,

the more I understood why he avoided work.

He just couldn't grasp the concepts.

I met with him at lunch one day and asked him about it.

"Hey, Amir, I've been trying to get you to do any work the last
few weeks, why aren't you trying?"
He shrunk.
"Because I can't do it," he said. "I'm dumb and no one will want
to be my friend anymore."
Kids can be really good at masking what they think are faults.
Adults too.
So as a teacher, it's our job to show how these things aren't
faults or deficits at all,
they're just a starting point to grow from.
Wouldn't you know it, once Amir understood everyone was in
different places,
he started doing work
and his friendships didn't change at all.
The only thing that changed
was his perception of himself.

Boots

My first year teaching, I had a sixth grader, Trenton,

who wore tall hiking boots all year round.

Winter, spring, summer, fall.

Boots, boots, boots.

Oftentimes, he spent more time fiddling with those boots than he

did writing in class.

One day, instead of writing, he was reworking the laces,

so I asked him about it.

"I can tell these boots are really important to you, Trenton," I said.

"What are they for?"

"They're field boots," he pointed out. "I'm gonna be a hunting guide

like my dad someday!"

It was said with such conviction it felt like the truth,

but the road we want to travel isn't always straight.

Years later, I ran into Trenton, who told me his story.

He said he went to college to be a graphic designer

and got his first job in retail,

but then ended up becoming,

you guessed it,

a hunting guide.

He said, "I wish I woulda just gone right to that, you know?

I wasted a lot of time doing things I didn't love,

and I love being a hunting guide."

There is a special presence about someone

who is doing exactly what they want to do.

There is a new light in their eyes.

So that's what I think about when I see hunting boots.

Sometimes we get distracted trying on all these different shoes,

when maybe we should've just stuck

with the same boots all along.

Painting

My third year teaching, I had a student named Ethan, who was

perhaps one of the most naturally talented artists I've ever met.

He was completely self-taught,

and he produced some mesmerizing pieces.

Intricately woven, painted lines that would result in such

a picture, it made you try to fathom how anyone could possibly

think so creatively.

I wish this story continued on that same positive trajectory,

but it does not.

The life surrounding Ethan was turbulent, to say the least.

Despite the best efforts by myself,

other teachers, and assistance programs,

Ethan's negative environment swallowed him

by the time he was in high school,

and he was never the same.

It is so difficult to watch someone's essence slip away like that,

especially when you are doing all you can to help.

It is absolutely heartbreaking.

That is what haunts me when I view paintings sometimes.

There was so much color to Ethan's potential

until it was all taken away from him,

completely out of his control.

No one deserves that outcome.

Not one,

especially a child.

Pencil Sharpener

My second year teaching, I had a student named Olivia

who took things apart.

When I say "apart," I mean break it down into each

individual piece.

She took apart my pens, microscopes,

even a drawer off my filing cabinet!

I was nervous that if I left the room, my own chair would

get dismembered.

She occasionally got into some trouble

because she never asked permission and rarely put things

back together,

but one day, I put Olivia's skills to the test.

My electric pencil sharpener wasn't

working

because another kid jammed a paper

clip in there,

so I contacted the only

expert I knew.

"Hey, Olivia," I said, tapping her on the shoulder.

"Think you can take this apart to see what is wrong?"

You would have thought I gave her a million dollars.

"Are you serious?!" she bounced. "Yes! I would love to!"

"Great, but there is a catch," I warned. "You have to try to put it back

together too."

Olivia paused to consider the arrangement.

"Well, I've never done that before," she hesitated. "But I'll try my best!"

She immediately took the entire thing apart,

fixed it,

and put it back together in less than ten minutes

while the class cheered her on the entire time.

Everyone deserves to have a moment like that.

When I see a pencil sharpener, that is what I think about.

Who hasn't had an opportunity to shine yet,

and how can we give them the chance?

Bent Straw

My fifth year teaching, we had a student named Dylan,

who was struggling in many areas of school.

He wasn't performing well academically,

his behavior was concerning,

and at the core of it all, he was just really angry.

We talked to his mom often

and even though she was very supportive,

we weren't seeing any changes in Dylan.

Ultimately, we asked his mom, Melissa, to come in for a meeting.

She arrived, slightly disheveled, holding a fast-food soft drink.

After we laid out his successes from the year,

we started to talk to her about Dylan's behavior and academics,

and that's when she took the straw out of the drink.

She moved it all around, bending it and stretching it as she spoke.

I don't think she was even aware she was doing it.

"I talk to him about these things at home, but nothing is changing,"

Melissa started.

"I just don't know how I'm going to do this all by myself."

"That's why we wanted to talk to you," I said.

"You're not alone. We will figure this out together."

That's when she dropped the bent straw and started crying.

Parenting is difficult, especially when you feel

like you don't have any strategies left.

I think we forget how many parents are figuring out parenting

for the first time,

and that can feel pretty overwhelming, especially if it's not going well.

Just because a child's behavior isn't changing

doesn't mean parents aren't doing anything about it.

Sometimes it just means they don't know what to do,

and that's an opportunity to show grace and

understanding

and offer help where we can.

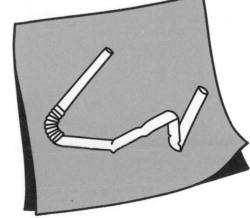

A Bike Seat

Toward the end of each summer, we do a sixth-grade orientation.

Students come to spend a day at school

to practice their locker,

meet their teachers,

and do some fun team-building

activities to meet new people.

I was doing check-in when a student

named Malachi rolled up on a bike,

but it didn't have a seat.

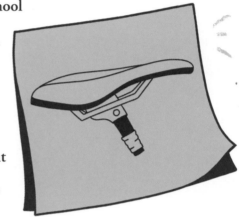

"Hey! My name is Malachi!"

he said excitedly. "Is school starting?!"

"Not yet, this is just orientation," I informed him.

"Did you sign up?"

"Probably not, my parents never know what is going on."

He glanced over his shoulder like he was looking at something

I couldn't see.

"Can I still come today?"

We were able to verify that Malachi was scheduled to be at this school,

but we couldn't get ahold of his parents.

Still, he got to stay for the day.

At the end, I watched him ride off on that bike,

without a seat.

When school started again, Malachi continued riding his bike to school.

Day after day.

No bike seat.

The school ended up calling Child Protective Services,

who discovered Malachi's parents were rarely home,

leaving eleven-year-old Malachi to figure things out on his own.

As a teacher, there is a constant struggle to figure out ways

to help motivate students to learn and participate,

especially in the past few years.

I even have trouble finding ways to motivate myself some days.

It's in those moments I think about Malachi.

A kid with little foundation or support

but somehow found the internal drive to get himself to school,

even if that meant riding a bike without a seat

all the way across town.

Wi-Fi Bars

My sixth year teaching, I had a student named Parker,

who was a technology genius.

I mean it.

A genius.

He built his own computers,

could fix any glitch,

and often had a workaround for every tech-related problem.

But he also got into trouble.

He kept bypassing the district's filters and playing video games on

his personal device during school, so one day, the district took it.

That is where the story begins.

The next day, Parker came up to me during work time and asked

me a question.

"What would happen if someone shut down the school's Wi-Fi?"

he said.

"What do you mean?" I asked. "Like on purpose?"

"Yeah, on purpose."

"I'm not sure," I admitted, "but I suppose they would get into trouble."

Parker shrugged and went back to his seat.

The next day when I got to work, the school's Wi-Fi was shut down.

I went to the principal immediately and told him about my conversation
with Parker.

Turns out it *was* Parker, and he got in a lot of trouble.

However, the school decided to lean into Parker's talents,

and he spent two hours a week in the tech department

learning more about computers

and, of course, the ethics within.

There are so many talented kids out there, some smarter than us already.

I can't look at Wi-Fi bars without

thinking of Parker

and how it's up to us to teach

kids how to navigate their talents

because who knows,

some of them might use them

to change the world.

A Bouncy Ball

I was grading papers one morning and received a call from the

office that one of my students, Kaylee, never showed up for art

class, and they were having trouble finding her.

I did some laps around my wing of the school

and ended up finding her tucked next to a locker in the corner.

She had her hood up

and was rolling a bouncy ball between her hand and the tile floor.

"Can I sit next to you?" I asked.

She scooted over to make some room.

"I am just having a hard day . . ." she began.

I was trying to think about what to say next,

but she noticed I was staring at the bouncy ball.

"I used to do this when I was younger," she said. "I like the way it

feels, I guess."

"I used to do things like that too," I said, motioning toward the

ball. "Can I try?"

And then we sat there for a while, taking turns rolling the ball

back

and forth

under our hands.

I know it sounds strange,

but when I started rolling that bouncy ball,

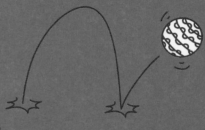

I jumped right into the soul of being a kid.

I could feel the weight of her day.

Truly feel it.

I can't hold a bouncy ball without taking a minute to roll it.

For some reason,

it connects me back to my own childhood memories,

where things seemed simple

and straightforward.

I think about this when I talk with other adults sometimes.

What is their bouncy ball,

and what was their childhood like?

Your Name

One of my students, Liam, had a hard transition to middle school.

He had a lot of things he needed to work on,

but the one that stood out the most was his motivation.

He seemingly just didn't care to do, well, anything.

No materials?

He shrugged it off.

Didn't do well on a test?

Didn't matter.

I tried so many things to help motivate this kid.

I tried involving parents.

I tried adjusting the material.

I tried having deep, meaningful conversations with him.

None of those strategies worked, until something did by accident.

We were studying Greek mythology, and many of those character names have meaning.

As a way to *try* and get Liam excited, I said, "Hey, Liam, have you ever looked up what your name means?"

"No. Why?"

"It's Irish, and it stands for strong-willed or determined warrior."

He was shocked like we unlocked a new part of his life.

"That's what my name means?!"

"It sure does," I said.

"Wait, that's *me*?!" he said, his excitement still growing. "This is awesome."

The next day and for many days after that,

Liam was noticeably different in class.

He participated in discussions, and his organization improved quite a bit.

It reminds me there are so many layers to who we are

and so many layers yet to be discovered too.

And who knows,

maybe the next thing that motivates you

might just be as simple

as rediscovering your own name.

Hair Ties and Yoga Pants

It was Dress Like a Superhero for spirit week.

So, when my sixth-grade student, Ananya, walked into class

wearing giant pink and purple yoga pants that could have fit me,

I knew there was a story behind it.

I didn't even get a chance to ask though,

because she came to me first in a panic.

"Mr. Eich, do you have something I could use to tighten the waist

on these?" she asked.

"I'm not sure," I said, looking around the room. "Maybe just roll

them up a bit to help?"

That wasn't the answer she was hoping for.

I could see her frustration was about to reach a boiling point,

but it didn't

because Taylor stepped in.

"Here, I have a hair tie you could use," she said.

Taylor removed the hair tie from her ponytail

and spent the next few minutes using it to bunch up the waist

of the yoga pants.

Each time she adjusted it to be a bit tighter,

you could see Ananya's shoulders drop a little bit more.

We often think of superheroes for those big moments, you know?

Where everything builds toward one giant moment of heroism.

I think we begin to believe that's what it has to look like.

But I like the smaller moments more.

The ones you might miss.

The ones that happen with no buildup

or extraordinary circumstances.

To me, discovering those moments gives me a better sense

of who I want to be,

even if it comes in the form

of some hair ties and yoga pants.

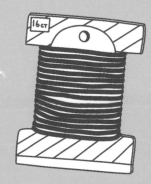

Microphone

Our school was hosting a variety show for a fundraiser.

Many students were volunteering to do a skit, perform a talent,

or sing a song.

Jordan, though, was hesitant.

"I want to sing," he admitted. "But I think I'll get too nervous."

His friends and other classmates were super encouraging.

"You can do it, Jordan!"

"Yeah! It'll be great."

So, Jordan signed up.

On the day of the show, Jordan stepped up to the microphone

in front of the audience.

He started off just fine,

but then

puberty arrived.

His voice squeaked,

then dropped

and squeaked again.

In fact, there wasn't a single pitch Jordan was able to match

with the melody.

I caught a glimpse of the crowd.

Jordan's classmates were frozen.

He finished the song and received a lovely applause,

but I was nervous Jordan felt embarrassed from his squeaks.

However, when Jordan joined his classmates, his reaction surprised me.

"Did you guys see me?!" he asked. "I made it through the whole thing!"

I kicked myself because I almost missed it.

I jumped right to what I thought success for Jordan should look like,

instead of what he was actually there to do.

So when I see a microphone, that's what I think about.

Measuring success is different for everyone,

and you can't be the judge of it.

Blue Ice Cream

One year, I had a student named Montaya who was a storyteller. She was super energetic and talked faster than any student I'd had up to that point.

"Hi Mr. Eich what did you do this weekend I had blue ice cream I was up north with my family and we went to go get ice cream but before that we went swimming in the lake and that was the first time because I never get in the water especially when . . ."

Her stories, well, they were never short. . . .

". . . especially when it's cold but that day was supposed to be eighty-six degrees, but it turns out it was eighty-nine degrees which doesn't seem like much of a change but three degrees is a lot when you are trying to stay warm when you get out of the water . . ."

But no matter the story I always listened.

". . . when you get out of the water and that's when my Dad said let's go get ice cream and first I wanted the blue flavor but blue isn't a flavor or maybe it is I don't know but I got the blue anyways."

It was after this story Montaya asked me a question.

"Mr. Eich, why do you listen to my stories?"

"Because they are important," I said. "That's why."

"Oh. Well, I know they get long, but I can tell you are always listening, and I'm glad about that."

Everyone has a story to tell, don't they?

And to be seen and heard is so essential

because that's how we learn about each other.

So that's what I think about when I see blue ice cream.

Everyone has a story to tell,

and those stories are important.

 Every. Single. One.

Big Muscles
and a Duck

We were doing an assessment over figurative language elements, and

two students, Erika and Steph, were cheating.

Like, clearly cheating.

Head over, looking at each other's test, and going back to their own.

I didn't want to disrupt the other students,

so I let them continue.

At the end of class, I had the two of them stay back

so we could discuss what happened,

but Erika started to talk instead of me.

"Are we in trouble for drawing during the test?" she asked.

"What do you mean," I said, confused. "What drawings?"

"The drawings on the test," she laughed. "You didn't see them?"

I went through the pile of tests and pulled theirs out.

On Erika's was an image of a person with huge muscles.

"It's you, Mr. Eich, 'cuz you always joke about how strong you are."

Then Steph chimed in:

"And when I saw her drawing it, I knew I had to make one too,

but I turned you into a duck

because of that story you told us the other day."

The two of them just kept giggling.

"Thank you," I said smiling. "You've really captured my best features."

It's sad how easily we can jump to conclusions, isn't it?

Luckily, this mistake guided me back to how I should treat not just kids,

but also, people in general.

And getting a self-portrait in the process was pretty cool too.

Rolling Dice

We were doing some get-to-know-you activities in the first month

of the year, and we were doing an obstacle course relay race.

Christopher was hyped.

"I love relays! Oh my gosh, I am so good at it too!" he boasted.

"You just watch me zoom!"

The moment I blew the whistle to start,

Christopher showed he was actually quite good at obstacle courses.

Like, it was crazy how far ahead he was.

However, at the end of the course, you have to roll a dice

and get it to land on the number six.

That is something that life wasn't going to allow Christopher to do

that day.

He rolled every number but a six for almost a straight minute.

"What is happening?!" he yelled. "Everyone is gonna pass me!"

Christopher ended up getting last place

and seemed a little defeated at first,

but then he had a smirk on his face.

"Hey! Listen up!" he said. "I might have lost, but you saw me

zoom though, right?! I zoomed!"

Everybody laughed.

That's how "I still zoomed!" became a positive saying

my students would shout out the rest of the year.

They even made a small poster

and stuck it to the wall.

There are definitely days where things don't go as planned,

and I feel like I am rolling every number but a six.

It can be extremely frustrating.

But if I sit and think of the process it took me to get to that point,

I just smile and think:

I still zoomed.

Time

It was the last day of school, and we were doing many

things to celebrate the end of the year.

We had a class picnic outside,

watched a slideshow with pictures from the year,

and played all the favorite class games.

Everyone seemed to be having a blast

except Theo.

He was participating, but there was no expression

on his face,

which was unusual,

because Theo wore his heart on his sleeve.

"Hey, Theo," I said. "Want to lead this next activity?"

"No," he shrugged. "I just want to watch it."

He was quiet for a second, then continued.

"How come when you don't want to be somewhere,

time goes slow,

but when you want to stay, time goes fast?"

"Is today a 'time goes fast' day?" I asked.

He nodded.

It's always interesting watching a student have an epiphany.

I've seen this quite a bit.

But there is a heaviness when it deals with time

because that is something no one can control.

I wasn't able to control time for Theo,

but we were able to pause our celebration at the end of the day

to make sure he got everyone's phone number

before the day was done.

Even though the day went too fast for Theo,

he has plenty of time left.

Unfortunately,

that isn't true for all of us,

which is why

time is so valuable.

Pizza Box Note

We celebrated our poetry unit by having a pizza party

where students got the chance to read their original poems.

It was amazing,

and the kids had a great time,

but I noticed Lucy sneaking some extra pieces of pizza

between two plates.

Before the end of the class, I was able to ask Lucy a question.

"Hey, Lucy, we have some pizza left over from earlier," I pointed out.

Would you like some?"

"Um . . . yes," she said, her eyes beaming. "How much can I have?"

"As much as you want," I replied.

"Can I have all of it?" she asked. "It's for my family."

We combined all the leftover pizza into one box and sent her on her way.

But that's only half the story.

I was out sick the next day.

When I returned and looked over my guest teacher's notes,

there was a line that said,

"Lucy wanted to make sure you got this."

On my desk was a torn piece of cardboard.

On one side was the pizza logo,

and on the other side was a handwritten note.

It said, "Thank you for the pizza last night, Mr. Eich."

I have received a lot of thank you notes in my time teaching,

but none quite like that.

We made sure to get Lucy's family connected with the help they needed,

but I can't look at a pizza box without thinking of her family

and the families still out there

who are still in need of help.

Shaving Cream

Niko came into class one day, and I could tell he had
a new aura of confidence.

"Hey, everyone!" he said, strutting into the room. "How's it goin'?"

He was walking especially tall and kept rubbing his upper lip.

As we began the lesson,

I could tell his mind was occupied with something else,

and I finally learned with what when he asked to go to the bathroom.

"Hey, Mr. Eich, you mind if I use the restroom really quick?" he asked.

I said sure and started to write him a pass, but he had more to say.

"You know, I started shaving yesterday," he announced.

"Oh, really?" I said, genuinely surprised. "That's a big milestone."

"Yeah, I know," he agreed. "So, I gotta go shave right now, you know
how it is."

"You are going to shave . . . right now?"

"Yeah, I've got shaving cream and an electric razor in my backpack just
in case," he said, pointing out to the hallway.

"And I can feel some hair coming in,

so I'm gonna take care of it real quick."

Then he walked out of the classroom walking even taller than before.

It's so fun to watch kids embrace the idea of getting older,

even as my own hair starts to turn gray.

I hope I don't lose sight of the joys that come with getting older,

even as an adult.

I might be getting older,

but there is so much joy ahead,

so, I walk

a little taller.

Silence and Stars

We were able to take our students to an overnight environment camp.

Many of our students have never left the city

or camped,

and we were going to take them to northern Minnesota

in the middle of winter.

There was some complaining at the beginning,

but by the middle of the day, everyone was having a blast,

including Joyce.

"Mr. Eich, this is so much fun!" she yelled during a hike. "I've never

done anything like this!"

That night, we took the kids on a hike on a frozen lake,

and we all spread out,

turned off our flashlights,

and laid down on the ice

in silence

while we stared up at the stars.

Complete silence.

When it was time to hike back, I noticed one student was still lying down.

It was Joyce.

"You ready to hike back?" I whispered.

"I didn't know what silence was until today," she said. "I'm gonna

miss this."

And then we just stood there, gazing up.

The rest of the class joined us,

so, we all stood there together

in the silence and stars.

We don't always get to choose what we remember,

but sometimes you can feel the powerful potential of a moment.

I think that was it for Joyce,

and I hope she remembers it forever

because I certainly will.

Picture Frame

It was the third week of school, and one of my students, Paxton, was

causing problems.

It's never a good thing when you hear other kids

telling you what Paxton did

before you see him,

but that was the reputation he was creating for himself.

One day, we were practicing skits students wrote.

Everyone was using different props I collected over the years.

But for Paxton,

it was too much stimulation.

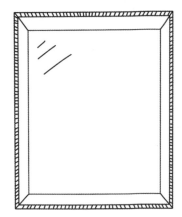

He was taking other groups' materials,

disrupting everyone,

and right as I was about to address it . . .

SNAP!

He stepped on a wooden picture frame,

breaking it in half.

The class froze to watch what would happen next.

I picked up the frame and started to see if it was worth repairing.

The class watched silently,

but not Paxton.

"Am I in trouble for breaking that?" he said unfazed. "Am I going to the

office or something?"

"No, the frame isn't important to me, Paxton," I said, "but you are.

I want you to be *here*,

not *there*."

Then class continued,

and Paxton was calmer,

but not by much.

What I've learned after years of teaching

is that genuine change requires genuine care.

Paxton had a lot more to learn,

but in that moment, he learned exactly what I needed him to know:

he is more important to me than things,

and that's a good place to start a solid foundation.

_____

Brownies

I was not having a good day.

My students weren't doing anything out of the ordinary,

but my patience limit was already maxed out.

I was up all night with my daughter who couldn't sleep,

our car battery had died, and I had to get a ride,

and none of my classroom technology was working,

so the lesson was doomed from the start.

On top of it all, I was not able to put on a happy face for my students,

and that gave me teacher guilt,

which made me even more miserable.

I don't even like thinking about it.

At lunchtime, one of my students, Arkell, came into my room.

He was holding a tray full of brownies.

"Hey, Mr. Eich, it seems like you're having a bad day," he pointed out.

"So, I got a bunch of kids to donate their brownies,

so now you have a brownie mountain!"

I don't think I've flipped from a frown to a smile so fast.

I actually felt better the rest of the day

until I got a bellyache from all the brownies I ate.

I think we often try to give people space

when we think they are in a bad mood,

but maybe that's not always the right move.

Maybe they just need to be given

a genuine dose of kindness to bring them back,

or you know,

a tray full of brownies couldn't hurt either.

The Green Jacket

The season was changing to fall, which meant I could start wearing

my favorite jacket:

a green fleece that fit me perfectly.

My classroom was also an ice box, so I wore it often.

One day, I noticed one of my students, Casey, kept staring at me.

She rarely spoke unless prompted, but at the end of the lesson

she asked me a question.

"Mr. Eich, can you give me a hug?" she asked while standing unusually

close to me.

As I went in to give her a hug,

she wrapped her arms around my waist,

latched her hands together in the back

and squeezed me tight.

She didn't let go.

It almost felt like a necessity.

When she finally released her grip, I didn't get to say anything,

because she turned around quickly and left.

I was left just standing there, wondering.

The next day, before students arrived, I got a phone call.

It was from Casey's mom.

She said her husband was recently deployed overseas,

and I was wearing the same jacket that her husband also owned.

"I am calling to let you know that whatever you did yesterday

sent Casey home happier than I've seen her in a while," she said

through tears.

"So, thank you."

Casey asked for many more hugs throughout the rest of the year,

and I don't know who the hugs helped more,

me or Casey.

When I wear this jacket, I am reminded of many things,

but mostly the feeling of a kid

who misses her dad

more than anything else.

Flannel Shirts

It didn't take long for me to figure out my student, Hannah, wore a

similar outfit each day:

Jeans and a button-up flannel shirt,

sometimes buttoned to the very top.

So, I was surprised to see when she came to school wearing something

completely different:

white sneakers,

long black leggings,

and a flowy top.

I watched her walk over to a group of girls who wore that same outfit

almost every day,

but Hannah looked *very* uncomfortable standing there.

Constantly fidgeting with the waist of the leggings

and fighting to keep the neck of her shirt over her shoulder.

Hannah joined the circle of girls,

but she never spoke to them,

and seemed a little down the rest of the day.

It's hard to watch kids make a decision that takes them away

from who they are,

but it's also uplifting when you see them succeed in the opposite.

The next day, Hannah came to school in her usual outfit.

She went to the same group of girls

and began talking to them without hesitation.

Before long, they were all talking with Hannah

and having a great time.

I think the assumptions we make about ourselves

tend to drive us to make decisions that take away who we are

when, instead, we should be like Hannah

and know that who we are

is enough.

And I hope you know that too.

Dented Water Bottle

A new water bottle fashion trend had taken over our middle school.

It doesn't matter the brand

because it's happened multiple times over my career.

There were the Hydro Flasks.

The YETIs.

The Stanleys.

That year, it seemed like everyone had a brand-new trendy water bottle,

fresh off the supply line.

But not Harper.

Harper's was clearly not new.

It had dents,

worn-out stickers,

and a series of half-made bracelets wrapped around the lid.

She caught me staring at it too.

"I know I probably need a new one," she laughed.

"But I like this one because I can tell you a story

about every single mark and sticker on it."

I pointed at the largest dent. "What's that one about?"

As Harper laughed while recounting a tale of a camping trip gone bad,

all I could do was smile along.

"It was crazy, Mr. Eich!" she said, arms in the air. "We got lost, and I

was crying,

but we finally found our way out! Isn't that wild?!"

There have been days where all I want is to start over.

Completely reset with something brand new, you know?

But what I don't want is to lose the adventure.

I want the stickers and the stories,

and when I get dented,

I want to be able to look back,

laugh and say,

"That was wild!"

Fire Alarm

My student, Skylar, was highly sensitive to noise.

Anything loud or unexpected would send him into a long, emotional panic.

So, when I saw the fire drill schedule for the year, I knew we needed a plan.

"Hey, Skylar," I said. "Come here, I want to show you something."

"Is it large headphones?!" he panicked. "I don't want to wear large headphones!"

"No, no," I assured him. "Check this out."

I quietly showed him a YouTube video of a fire alarm.

You could barely hear it.

"We have fire drills coming up this year," I reminded him. "I know those can make you nervous."

"No," he corrected. "They make me cry."

"Okay, well, I was thinking we could listen to this a little bit louder every day," I suggested. "Do you want to try?"

So, every morning for weeks, my day started

listening to a fire alarm with Skylar.

Louder.

And LOUDER.

AND LOUDER!

Until Skylar was the one choosing the volume.

When the actual fire drill happened, Skylar cried but just a few tears, and

then said something that would stick with me forever.

"Mr. Eich, I *almost* did it! I only cried a little!"

I think sometimes when we face challenges,

we think it should take one big action to conquer them.

But in most cases, it's the persistence and the mini-challenges

you win along the way

that you should be proud of too

because that's where growth occurs.

You can't let "almost" fool you

because sometimes "almost" is pretty darn good.

Just ask Skylar.

Triple Hearts

One year, we had triplets in our grade.

Joshua, Josiah, and Jacob.

It took me about two weeks to tell them apart and get their names right.

They were gracious and only messed with me a few times.

"Mr. Eich!" one of them said. "Who am I?!"

"You're Jacob," I said confidently. "Because your hair is parted
in the middle."

"Nope! I'm Joshua!" he laughed. "I parted my hair down the middle
to trick ya!"

But one day, when they weren't fooling me,

Jacob tripped over a chair

and broke his finger.

I'm not giving details.

It was clearly broken.

It took me a few minutes to calm him down enough to get him to his

feet, and when I finally did, I turned around to see two kids

in the doorway.

It was Josiah and Joshua, and they were alert.

"Is Jacob okay?!" they blurted. "What happened?!"

"He'll be okay," I assured them, "but I need to take him to the nurse."

As the four of us walked down the hallway together,

I suddenly realized that I didn't know why Josiah and Joshua came

to my room in the first place.

"Why did you guys come to my class?" I asked. "You're supposed to

be in math."

Joshua didn't hesitate to answer.

"We have triple hearts, Mr. Eich," they announced. "We could feel

something was wrong."

It's moments like these that make me wonder

about the depth of human connection.

Maybe our hearts are more connected than we realize,

and we are never really far away

from the ones we love.

Bubble Gum

One of my students, Dustin, was quite popular.

Every morning, he was surrounded by kids.

A giant crowd, with Dustin at the center.

Why, you might ask?

Well, Dustin had a bag of bubble gum.

And he was handing it out . . .

for free.

Now, if you don't work in a middle school,

you should know that handing out free candy

is going to get you the most attention

you've ever received in your life.

Dustin did this every morning.

Handing out gum wasn't a problem,

but what I saw every moment after was.

Dustin was always left alone.

Always.

The candy was gone, and so was the crowd.

I brought this observation to Dustin one day,

but he didn't quite understand.

"So you think I should give them candy throughout the day

instead of all at once?" he asked.

"No, I was wondering what would happen if you brought in some-

thing that represented something you like to do," I suggested.

"You could bring in your skateboard or—"

"My baseball cards!" he blurted. "Do you think anyone else

collects those?!"

"I bet if you bring those in tomorrow, you will find out," I said.

The next day, Dustin showed up with some of his cards,

and a few kids were interested in talking.

The day after those kids brought in their cards.

By the end of the month, every morning at school, Dustin no

longer had a crowd.

He now had connections,

and he was never alone.

Notebook

We were about a week into our poetry unit.

We spent the first week analyzing poetry

and also learning about all the literary elements that go along with it,

but now it was time to create.

After a full day of writing, I saw Remy's notebook was empty,

so I asked her about it.

"Hey, Remy, I noticed you didn't write anything down yet."

"I keep trying," she informed me, "but right when I start, I stop."

"Oh, what is stopping you?" I asked.

"I just keep thinking about how bad it will be," she sighed, "and how no one will like it."

It's hard watching self-doubt creep into someone's creative spirit, especially a kid.

As someone who loves to create, I feel this occasionally as well, but I've learned to counter it.

"Hey, Remy, what's the best thing that could happen if you write this poem?" I asked.

"Umm . . . I get a good score?" she guessed.

"Sure, but what else?"

"Umm . . . people might like it?"

"And?" I said, pushing for more.

"And maybe I'll like it too?"

"That sounds pretty good, doesn't it?"

Remy nodded, and a few minutes later,

I saw her jotting things down in her notebook.

Not too long after that, Remy asked if she could show a friend her poem.

We all have blank pages.

Some are actually in notebooks, but others are somewhere else.

That is a lot of room for some incredible possibilities.

All you need to do is get started.

Locker

I had a student, Raina, who was in a large foster care home.
We were told about her situation before the school year even started
because we knew she was going to need a lot of support from multiple
people in the building.
She missed locker move-in day,
so on the first day of school, I made sure to find her right away.
"Hey, Raina, my name is Mr. Eicheldinger," I said. "We are going to
have a lot of fun,
but first, I want to get you set up with a locker."
Raina gave me a slight smile,
and we opened her locker together.
She stared at it for a moment.
"Is this locker just for me?" she asked. "I don't have to share it?"
"Just yours," I confirmed. "It's all for you."
Raina took a minute and continued to stare at the locker.
"I've never had something I didn't have to share. Can you help me
decide where to put things?"

We spent the next few minutes putting things in.

Carefully,

purposefully.

Sometimes during the year,

I would catch Raina standing in front of her open locker

making small adjustments to its contents

but with purpose.

We all need a place to call our own,

especially when we are growing up.

For Raina,

it was a locker.

It might have been small,

but for her,

it was more than she'd ever had.

Painted Turtles

My class was studying together for an assessment.

Everyone was in groups reviewing using different resources,

except for Lola.

She had a book about turtles on her desk

and a small wooden turtle sitting on top of it.

To be clear,

we were *not* studying anything about turtles.

"Hey, Lola, I see you are looking at turtles," I said.

"They are painted turtles," she politely corrected. "And I want to learn
about them."

"That's awesome, Lola," I said. "But I also don't want you to miss this
study session though."

Lola got flustered almost immediately.

"But when am I going to learn
about turtles?! I have piano and
soccer practice!"

She looked around in a panic.

"When do I get to learn what I want to learn?"

It's never easy when obligations and responsibilities collide with desires.

It can be a tricky balance to navigate for kids and adults alike.

"Okay, Lola, how about this," I suggested.

"Today, you and I study. But tomorrow, during reading time,

let's learn about turtles together."

"It's a deal, Mr. Eich," she said, and we shook hands.

It just so happens that turtles are my favorite animal,

but after that day, I view them a bit differently.

You don't always have to give up your desires for responsibility;

sometimes you just need to get creative

and view time not as a limit

but instead as a path

that will put you right where you were meant to be.

Football Helmet

One of my students, Blake, came into class wearing a football helmet.

I figured there was a story, and Blake immediately filled me in,

but he said it all in one breath.

"Before you say I have to take it off I want you to know I want to wear

this all day because football players are strong, and this helmet is heavy

so if I wear it I'll get stronger and it will help the team and maybe

they'll see me wearing it and inspire them to get strong."

"Sounds good," I reassured him. "As long as you are learning and it's not

distracting, it doesn't matter to me what you wear."

So Blake wore the helmet,

but not for as long as I thought he would.

I was helping another student when I heard it hit the ground,

and Blake was in the corner

crying.

"I can't do it!" he wailed. "The helmet hurts and I'm not strong enough,

my coach is going to be so disappointed!"

The feeling of disappointing others can be a tough one.

But sometimes I think we put that pressure on ourselves

when it isn't necessary.

"You know what Blake," I encouraged, "I bet your coach will actually

be really proud of you."

"Why?" he asked, sniffling through tears.

"Because you made the choice to work hard for the team, even when

the coach wasn't watching. So here is what I am going to do. . . ."

I wrote a quick note to Blake's coach,

letting him know I witnessed Blake's team-minded approach

and that I was very proud.

I don't know about you,

but if I'm on a team with anyone,

I'd want it to be with someone like Blake

because those are the people that will lift you up

to a higher place.

Sticks

We were out on a nature hike during a beautiful fall day in Minnesota.

But I wasn't looking at the leaves much,

because I was focused on Lucia.

I'd received an email from her parents earlier that week

informing me they were getting a divorce

and that their daughter, Lucia, was having a hard time with the news.

Some kids are pretty good at hiding their emotions.

Lucia was not one of them.

She was in the back of the line

holding a long, thin stick,

so I decided to join her.

"I'm guessing you already know about my parents," she started.

"Yes, they let me know," I admitted. "Is that something

you want to talk about?"

"I just don't understand it," she said, pushing the stick into the dirt.

"That's all."

During my time as a teacher,

I've seen many students go through big family changes.

Each situation is unique,

but the response from the kid is very much the same in one way.

They have a lot of questions.

"I know it's hard to understand right now," I said.

"But I guarantee your parents love you, without question."

"Without question?" she said.

"Yes," I replied, "without question."

I picked a stick off the ground and started to tap hers.

In a matter of seconds, we were laughing and swordfighting

as we caught back up to the rest of the group.

I love my family so much, and that's how I see my students.

They are family, and they are loved,

without question.

Sandpaper

One of my former students, Alex, a senior, came back to complete his

Eagle Scout project.

For his project, Alex wanted to build picnic tables outside for students

to use at lunch,

and the principal said he could.

It just so happens that was the year I had a classroom with windows,

and it looked out onto the courtyard

where Alex was building them.

So every day,

for about a week,

my class got to watch Alex build.

When he was finally done, Alex got to take a picture alongside the tables

with some of my students for the local paper, and he was thrilled.

But the tables didn't stay nice long at all

because a few days later,

someone vandalized them with spray paint.

Long streaks of green, all over the top.

—

It was heartbreaking.

A few days later, when I got to school and opened the blinds

of my classroom window,

I saw one of my students, Tarun, sitting at one of the picnic tables.

He had a piece of sandpaper,

and he was trying his best to remove the graffiti.

He showed up every morning and sanded the table

until the graffiti was gone.

There was no crowd to watch him.

There was no prize or award.

It was just Tarun

and some sandpaper.

Now usually I like to end a story with something I've learned,

but some stories should just stand on their own

and this

is one of them.

Crayons

It was the final week of school, and right before I was about to leave for the day,

a group of seniors showed up in my doorway.

I recognized one of them right away.

It was Elise.

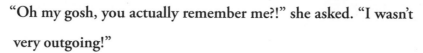

"Elise!" I exclaimed. "It is so good to see you!"

My response clearly caught her off guard.

"Oh my gosh, you actually remember me?!" she asked. "I wasn't very outgoing!"

"Of course I do!" I said. "How are you?!"

We spent the next few minutes recapping what she'd been up to the last few years,

her plans after graduation,

but at the end, there was an awkward pause

when she asked me a question.

"Mr. Eich, do you remember when you used to randomly put a crayon on my desk sometimes?"

"Um . . . I think so?" I said, slightly baffled.

"I loved the smell of crayons," Elise continued. "And you knew that.

So sometimes during class, you would just walk by

and put a crayon on my desk and give me a smile.

That was always the best part of my day."

I've tried my best over the years to have powerful and meaningful

moments with kids.

Sometimes it's through a large gesture.

Sometimes it's a one-on-one conversation.

And for the most part, I think those have worked.

But more recently I've really begun to understand the impact

of the tiny details.

The ones I barely remember

like the crayon.

It's those actions you think are so insignificant and small

that end up being what defines you.

It can be a little scary to think about

but also pretty darn awesome at the same time.

Tuba

One of my students, Carly, was struggling.

You see, Carly was shorter than most sixth graders,

but she played the largest instrument:

the tuba.

Most days you could hear Carly before you saw her

because that tuba case wasn't exactly quiet

as it clanged against the tile floor and lockers.

BANG! BANG! BANG!

By the time Carly and her tuba got to class,

she looked like she'd been in a wrestling match.

One day, curiosity got the best of me,

so I asked Carly a question.

"What inspired you to play the tuba?"

Carly shot me a look of confidence.

"I was told to play something smaller, but I don't want to," she insisted.

I want to play something *big* because I can."

I've definitely had plenty of moments where people underestimate me,

and that can hurt.

But you have to remember you don't need anyone's approval

to do what inspires you most.

You just need you.

And if for some reason you are questioned why you think you can do it,

I'd respond like Carly.

"Because I can."

Giant Sweatshirt

It was a cold winter day in Minnesota, and my sixth-grade students

were settling into class.

However, it looked like Nasir

had already had an adventure that morning.

His light gray sweatshirt was completely covered in chocolate milk,

and you could tell he was embarrassed,

so I pulled him aside.

"Hey, Nasir, want to see if the nurse has some backup clothes?" I asked.

"No," he said, and stuck his tongue out in disgust. "They only have

weird stuff."

I couldn't really argue with Nasir on that one.

Luckily, I keep a bunch of spare clothes in my classroom

because I constantly spill on myself throughout the day.

So, I offered Nasir a giant blue sweatshirt,

which he gladly accepted.

He wore it the rest of that day

even though the sweatshirt reached his knees.

He wore it the next day.

The next one too.

And possibly the rest of his life

because I never got it back,

but that's okay.

We give part of ourselves to people every day, don't we?

We give our patience,

our love,

and occasionally,

a sweatshirt.

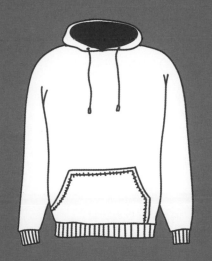

A Dream

I lost myself one day.

It had been a really frustrating day at work.

I could go into all the details of what makes a day frustrating

for a teacher,

but it's not worth it.

Just know that everything,

and I mean *everything*,

went wrong.

At the peak of it all, I lost myself.

I overreacted to a situation in my classroom,

and the class went silent.

I went silent too,

and I had to stay that way because I was so angry.

That night, I had a dream.

It was me,

alone in my classroom,

but I was watching myself walk around.

What I saw was a defeated, tired looking version of myself.

As the dream continued,

I watched myself go to each desk,

place my hand gently upon it,

and then go to the next one.

When I woke up, I knew what I needed to do.

When my students all arrived the next day,

I had them form a circle in the front of the room,

and I apologized.

It's hard to admit when you've made a mistake,

but you have to

because if you don't,

the trust erodes from the very thing you spent so much time creating:

a connection to the ones you care about the most.

Mario

It was the first day of school,

and a student entered my classroom wearing all Mario merchandise.

His shirt had Mario,

his pants had Mario,

and, of course, his backpack had it too.

He didn't waste any time introducing himself,

but he made me work for it.

"You will never guess what my name is!" he bragged. "Guess it!"

I'll save you the back and forth.

His name was Mario.

And Mario wore Mario stuff every day of the week.

Every.

Single.

Day.

Until one day, he wasn't.

There was no Mario on Mario,

and I could tell it was bothering him.

I quickly drew a little cartoon version of Mario (the student),

grabbed some tape,

and went to see him.

"I made you a video game version of yourself if you want to wear that

today instead," I offered.

"Wait, for real?!" he said. "I can wear this?!"

"Yes, but just so you know, I love playing *Super Mario* video games, but I

think you are the best Mario I know."

We can get lost in who we think we are

or

who we think we should be.

But your identity is so much more than what you like

or what you choose to wear.

There is a quiet essence to you that no one can repeat,

and we can find comfort in that too.

Coffee Mug

I had to run to the restroom in the middle of class.

Any teacher knows leaving your room, even for a few minutes,

can be a disaster.

So, I quickly did my business,

but when I returned, I found my coffee mug was tipped over,

and there was coffee all over my computer.

After I cleaned up the mess, I looked over at my class.

It was clear they knew what happened.

"I'm not mad or anything," I announced,

"but I'm guessing you all know how this happened, right?"

Silence.

Later that day, one of my students, Maisy, pulled me aside.

"Mr. Eich, I was the one who spilled your coffee," she admitted.

"I was just trying to get a pencil from your desk. . . ."

Honesty and truth:

two things I really struggled with as a kid.

So that's why you have to call it out when you see it,

even if it's a little later than you wanted it to be.

"Well, I guess I learned two things, Maisy," I said.

"What did you learn?" she said hesitantly.

"I learned you have an honest soul," I smiled. "And I probably

shouldn't keep my pencils anywhere near my coffee."

Would I have liked to know right away who spilled my coffee?

Sure.

But I don't want them to remember the mistake;

I want them to remember what it felt like

to tell the truth.

Seven Minutes

One of my students, Quinten, was on the track team,

and he was so excited.

I was one of the coaches, so I got to watch him dabble in all the events

and the first practices, but he finally landed on what he wanted to do.

The mile.

His first race, he ran a mile in seven minutes and fifteen seconds and

immediately set a new goal.

"I'm gonna break seven minutes in the mile," he said, determined.

"I know I can do it."

The next meet Quinten ran seven minutes and three seconds.

The meet after that, Quinten led the entire race and got seven minutes,

about as close as he could get to his goal.

In the final meet of the year, Quinten tried to take the lead again,

but he got cut off and drifted to the back.

A lap later, he tried to surge to the front,

but his feet got caught up with another runner,

and he fell to the track.

But he picked himself back up, caught the group,

fought his way to the front over the next two laps,

and won the race!

His time? Seven minutes.

This time, Quinten didn't come see me after the race.

I managed to find him in the middle of the field.

"I didn't get it, Coach. I ran a horrible race."

I disagreed.

"Quinten . . . you didn't just run today, you *raced*. You should be

extremely proud of yourself."

But some hearts cannot be contained.

Quentin asked if he could run one last time the next day.

I'm sure you'd love to know the time he got,

but I would ask you what is more important:

the time he got

or the journey to step on the track

one more time.

Sushi

I was in the cafeteria watching students eat lunch

(because being a teacher means you wear not just a couple of hats

but ALL of them).

One of my students, Lin, was carrying in

a few large Tupperware containers.

I shouted a joke his way, "Hey, Lin, are you feeding everyone today?"

He pivoted and came up to me right away.

"A bunch of my friends said they had never tried sushi and had a lot

of questions," he informed. "So I brought them all one

of their own so they could try it."

My face had to contort because I couldn't handle

the amount of kindness he was displaying.

"Do you want some too, Mr. Eich?" he continued.

So I sat with Lin as he passed out sushi to all his friends,

and he explained how he made it with his grandmother

because it was a family tradition.

What is unique about this story, though, are two things:

obviously, Lin's kindness and willingness to give.

But don't forget his friends either,

because they came with genuine curiosity too.

Put those together,

and what do you get?

An inclusive experience

where someone got to share part of their culture,

and it was celebrated by others.

What is better than that?

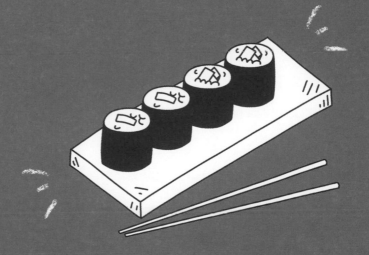

Phillip

I received a phone call from a parent during my prep.

She said, "Hi, Mr. Eich. Our family dog, Phillip, just passed away,

so we want to pick up Jeremiah instead of him taking the bus.

Can you let him know where to go for pickup?"

"Absolutely," I responded. "I am so sorry to hear what happened."

At the end of the day, I went to Jeremiah

and let him know his parents were picking him up.

He looked up at me and said, "Phillip died, didn't he, Mr. Eich?"

What people don't understand about teaching

is that heavy moments like this occur more often than you would think,

and each one requires something different.

I was trying to quickly decide what to say next,

but Jeremiah's friend spoke first.

"I'll walk with you to the car and wait with you," he said.

"You can tell me all about Phillip too."

Then the two of them left together.

Sometimes I think it's up to me to manage everyone's emotions—

to jump right in and protect them at all costs.

But moments like this remind me

the world is filled with so many wonderful people,

and if I jump in too quickly and try to take control,

I deny the opportunity for those individuals

to experience the joy of helping someone

who truly needs it.

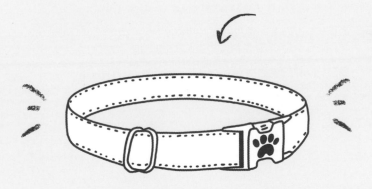

Shield

We were doing a get-to-know-you activity

a few weeks after school started.

I had never done it before, so a colleague quickly taught me the lesson.

Students were going to make these small shields

and decorate them with items about themselves and their families,

which would kind of be like a family crest.

The project started okay but quickly went downhill.

If you do an art project with kids

and *don't know* all the intricacies of that project . . .

it's doomed from the start.

The kids were confused,

the project was messy,

I was stressed,

and the majority of the shields didn't even look like shields by the end.

So needless to say,

we did not try the project again, ever.

Six years later, I was attending a graduation party for Diego,

and I went to my favorite part of these celebrations:

the picture timeline.

Diego had all these pictures from soccer

and family gatherings,

but then I noticed a picture of him in his room with his friends.

They were all wearing the cap and gowns from graduation.

That's when I saw it.

Over his shoulder on his shelf, displayed right in the center

was the shield from sixth grade.

We can experience so much of life

in a space where we make predictions

for how actions will affect others,

and we usually think of it as truth.

My memory of the shield lesson wasn't great,

but Diego's was much different.

That's the cool thing about moments and memories.

We might share an experience together,

but that doesn't mean we take the same thing away from it.

Waffles

One of my students, Rebecca, invited me to their specialty class to try

a new waffle recipe.

I am not one to turn down free food, especially breakfast.

So, the next day, I came to her class,

and all the waffles were laid out by the students.

Let's just say they varied greatly in appearance.

Rebecca saw me and brought a waffle over.

"I call this 'Celebration Surprise,'" she announced.

"You eat it after you win a big game, and it has a surprise inside!"

"That's awesome, Rebecca," I said. "So, what's inside?"

"You'll have to try it and see!" she laughed. "Go on! Taste it!"

I took a bite of Celebration Surprise,

and it was surprising, to say the least.

"So, what do you think, Mr. Eich?" Rebecca said with great anticipation.

"Do you like it?"

Feedback can be hard sometimes,

especially when the other person is eager to receive it.

So, you have to pair honesty with hope

and be invested in the results too.

"Rebecca, this is a great start, but for me it has too much of something . . ."

"Too much surprise?"

"Yes," I agreed. "Too much surprise. Do I get to try version two though?!"

"Absolutely! Come back tomorrow, and I'll have it ready to go!"

I ate a lot of Celebration Surprise waffles that week,

and they kept getting better.

But my favorite version was the original

because I got to see where it all started.

We rarely get to witness that:

the start of something new.

So, I try to treat every moment

like it could be the beginning

of something incredible.

Zipper

It was the middle of a long Minnesota winter.

One of my students, Sonja, walked to school every day.

Rain or shine.

And today happened to be an extra cold one.

When she walked into my room, she looked really disappointed,
and let me know right away.

"Mr. Eich, the zipper on my winter jacket broke, and I have to walk
home today," she grumbled.

"Do you think you could fix it?"

That was the start to the zipper battle I will never forget.

I worked on it in the morning,

over my lunch,

during my prep,

even during class when students were working!

A student named Hamza noticed my frustration and asked about it.

"Why are you working on that jacket so much, Mr. Eich?"

I told her the story while I kept fidgeting with the zipper,

but I could not get the thing reattached.

At the end of the day, I let Sonja know I was not able to fix it.

That's when Hamza stepped in.

"I get picked up today Mr. Eich," she said, "So Sonja could wear

my jacket home. I have another one at home I can wear tomorrow."

I watched Hamza as she led Sonja to her locker

and showed her all the cool pockets on her winter jacket,

which included a functional zipper.

I often wonder what makes us pause in a situation

where we could help someone

when instead, we could just be like Hamza.

See the need,

realize your opportunity to help,

and then

just do it.

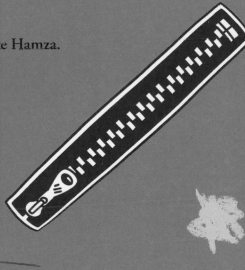

Halloween

It was the day before Halloween, which meant I was gearing up to teach

kids whose primary food intake for the next week would be candy.

There was a lot of energy in the school, especially from Markus.

"I love Halloween!" he yelled. "I love it!"

He even drew a map of the different neighbors he was going to visit

and the plans he had for all the candy.

"I'll probably have enough candy to last me until next Halloween,"

he boasted. "I can't wait!"

I expected to hear about his candy loot the following day,

but that is not what happened.

Turns out, Markus wasn't at school the next day

because he was struck by a car during his outing,

which resulted in a head injury and a stay in the hospital.

I was able to tell the class about it the next day,

and you can guess what they wanted to do.

My class brought in the most candy

I had ever seen collected in one place.

I needed three printer paper boxes to store it all

until Markus's parents came to pick it up.

You would think this story is over,

but it is not.

The same day that it was delivered to Markus,

I received a picture from his parents.

It was Markus in a wheelchair,

and he was delivering candy to all the kids

in the children's wing of the hospital.

I used to be surprised by actions like this,

but not anymore.

Because one of the unique abilities of children

is they can take an opportunity you think will be good,

and they somehow always find a way

to make it better.

Watch

I was an assistant coach for the girls' high school track and field team.

This particular day was an interval day,

which meant our athletes were going to run intervals

of two hundred meters; a total of ten.

Before we began, I noticed one of our athletes, Nadia, was

being comforted by others.

A teammate saw me staring and filled me in.

"Nadia failed her AP Chem test today, *and* got dumped by her

boyfriend," she said.

The girls lined up for their workout

and got their watches ready to time themselves.

Except for Nadia because she threw her watch on the ground.

Now, the thing about this workout is if you run the first few

too fast,

you'll burn out and won't be able to finish.

You *need* a watch.

———

The girls took off running.

They should run the first one in thirty-six seconds.

Nadia did hers in thirty-five.

She did the second one in thirty-four.

The third in thirty-four,

The fourth in thirty-one,

The fifth in twenty-eight.

Nadia then collapsed into the grass, unable to do more.

I knelt down next to her.

"I am here if you need me, okay?" I said. "That's all I want to tell you right now."

Nadia sat up, a little teary-eyed. "I just wanted to go until I couldn't anymore. I needed to."

There are plenty of times when I want to jump in and help or give advice on how to navigate life, but I also believe you shouldn't do that every time.

Sometimes you just have to let kids know you are there and allow them to handle it themselves, even if that means letting them run until they can't run anymore.

Magic

Nolan was adamant about showing us his magic trick one day.

"Please, Mr. Eich," he begged. "Let me do it at the end of class, please?!"

At the end of class, I had Nolan show us his trick,

but first, he had to establish his character.

"I, the great and powerful Nolan, will choose a card you are thinking

about!"

He pointed at a kid in the front row, "I know that *this* is the card you

are thinking about!"

But it wasn't.

So, Nolan did this, again, the following day.

"I, the great and powerful Nolan, will choose your card!"

And he tried this every day for weeks

with the same enthusiasm and energy,

no matter the outcome

(which was the same).

Finally, whether it was luck or magic,

Nolan chose a card that someone was thinking of,

and the class cheered.

"I did it! Mr. Eich! Did you see?!" he exclaimed. "They liked my magic!"

They may have,

but I think he missed the point,

so I let him know.

"Nolan, they did like your magic, but that's not why they watched.

They watched because they like you."

We get caught up in what we want to prove or show to others

like it will somehow define our reputation or perception of others.

When in reality, the magic people are looking for is really just you.

That's it.

Just you.

Handprints

My students and I decided to make a giant poster

to celebrate all the secretaries in the building.

We had trouble coming up with ideas,

but we finally settled on a "high five" design

and got to work right away.

I grabbed some finger paint

(a key craft ingredient for any teacher),

and over the course of the day,

all 130 of my students made their handprints

on a long piece of rolled-out paper.

We used all different colors too.

Purple

and green

and blue

and yellow.

After my students left for the day,

I brought the paper back into my room to dry,

and I had a moment.

I was looking at all these handprints.

From a distance,

they all looked similar.

But up close,

each one was unique.

I started thinking about all the handprints

the kids in the world could make, you know?

That's a lot of kids.

And they deserve our best

for everything.

Our absolute best.

Cornfield Maze

One fall afternoon, we took our students to an apple orchard.

Besides picking apples,

there were a variety of activities for the kids,

including a cornfield maze.

I watched as students got into groups to begin the maze,

but one of my students, Alejandro, was still standing at the start.

"Hey, Alejandro, are you thinking about doing the maze?" I asked.

"Nah, I'm not very good at mazes and know I'll get lost," he said.

"So I'm just gonna wait for everyone."

Confidence is a tricky thing, isn't it?

Even when the stakes seem low,

we can talk ourselves out of a lot of opportunities.

Another one of my students, Meghana,

came out of the start of the maze.

"Alejandro, I can't find the exit," she informed. "Can you help me?"

"But I don't know the way, either!" he said.

There are a lot of ways to help others in life.

You can lead them through it,

you can give them directions,

but I also think there is a large benefit

in joining them on the journey.

Alejandro and Meghana entered the maze together,

and a little while later,

made it out together.

"Mr. Eich! Can we do the maze again?!" they said. "Do we have time?!"

Life is funny like that.

Sometimes getting lost is the best way to build confidence in yourself,

and it doesn't hurt to have someone to get lost with either.

Dried Flowers

It was only a month into the school year,

and I was still getting to know my students.

One morning, I noticed one of my students, Melissa, was

spending a lot of time shoving something

in the clear plastic cover of her binder.

"Hey, Melissa, what are you working on?" I asked.

She flipped over her binder,

and I had never seen anything like it.

"These are dried flowers from all the hikes I've done with my

mom," she pointed out. "Every time we go on a hike,

I find a flower, bring it back home, and then dry it."

"Wow, Melissa," I said, truly impressed with the craft. "That's

incredible!"

"Yeah! I thought it would be cool

to put them in my binder like this

'cuz it reminds me of all the places I've been. Want to hear about one?!"

"Yes," I said. "I'd love to!"

One of the things I think is fascinating about being a human

is we spend so much energy trying to capture moments in time.

But I think we sometimes forget that sharing memories with others

helps us rediscover the joy of that original moment

and how it was meant to be remembered.

So that's what I think about when I see dried flowers.

Moments,

frozen in time,

just waiting to be rediscovered.

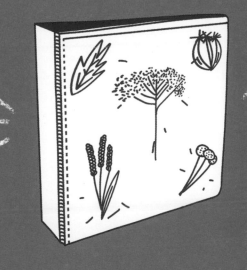

Tie

My students were preparing to give speeches to the class.

The topic was straightforward: a how-to speech.

You could demonstrate or explain how to set up a tent,

the best way to practice a slap shot,

basically anything, as long as you can explain the step-by-step process.

I have 130 students in any given year,

so it can be hard for me to keep track of what everyone is doing

all the time.

Which is why I was a little caught off guard when Otto presented

because he changed his topic from his original one.

He stood up in front of the class wearing dress pants

with a tucked-in button-up shirt that was way too big for him,

and resting on his shoulder was a loose tie.

"Hello everyone," he started, standing perfectly straight.

"Today, I am going to show you how to tie a tie. First, you need to . . ."

Otto froze.

He looked at me and whispered, "Mr. Eich, can I watch something on

my phone really quick?"

"Yes, if it will help," I encouraged. "Watch it over here by my desk."

Otto pulled the phone out of his pocket and started watching the video.

The video was of Otto filming his dad and grandpa.

The dad was sitting in a chair,

and Otto's grandpa was talking through how to tie the tie

as he demonstrated it on his son.

At one point in the video, I caught the reflection of Otto

in the bedroom mirror

as he watched his dad and grandpa.

He was just smiling.

I went home that day and sat on the floor with my daughters

as they giggled and played with their toys.

There is so much I want my girls to know and learn,

and I hope they smile as big as Otto

as I show them the best I can.

Making Moves

There was a buzz among many of my students because that night was

the final night for baseball tryouts.

"Dude, I'm gonna make the A team for sure!" one kid said.

"And I'll be a starting pitcher, of course," I overheard another say.

One of my students, Barrett, had his heart set on making

that top team too.

"I've been working hard, Mr. Eich, so I think I got a really good shot."

A few days later, the kids came to school,

and the tone among all of them was different,

and I already could guess why:

they must have released the results from tryouts.

There were many kids who were just as pumped as before.

"I'm on the A team again!" one said. "I told you I'd make it."

Unfortunately, Barrett didn't have that same energy,

but what he did have, I will never forget.

During class that day, Barrett was writing in his notebook

instead of reading,

"Hey, Barrett, what are you up to?" I asked.

"I didn't make the A team, so I'm making a list of the things I need

to do to get better," he said. "I'm making moves next year Mr. Eich.

I'm making moves."

In the face of disappointment after a long buildup of suspense,

it can be really easy to slip into a place

where you can't see your own dreams anymore.

But what we need to remember is believing in yourself,

as hard as it can be sometimes,

is the first step to achieving whatever it is that you want to do.

This is how failure works too.

You are still making moves toward your goal.

Sometimes you just don't realize it until much later.

Chain-Link Fence

I decided to take my students outside to catch some sun since
we had just finished a long writing assessment.
One of my students, Leo, was trying to climb
the chain-link fence of the tennis court.
"Leo, that's not an option!" I informed. "It's too high! Time to
get down."
Leo didn't feel like listening though
and continued to climb.
"Leo, I really don't want you to get hurt," I yelled. "Please
come down."
But Leo insisted he keep going.
"I'm good, Mr. Eich! I'm gonna climb *over* it!" he yelled.
"Check this out."
By now, Leo had the attention of the majority of the class
as he reached the top,
but as he swung his leg over to the other side,
something happened that Leo didn't expect.

The waistline of his pants snagged on the top,

which resulted in a wedgie

courtesy of the chain-link fence.

His pants were almost halfway up his back.

"Mr. Eich! I'm stuck!!!" he whined. "What should I do?!"

It's really hard to climb when you are trying not to laugh,

but I managed to get to the top

and unhook Leo's pants to help him down.

There are situations where a lecture is required.

This was not one of them.

I'm sure the wedgie was way more impactful

than my words would ever be.

Doorframe

It was open house at school, which is my absolute favorite.

I love seeing families come in, the excitement in the air, and of course,

the first impression I get from my new students.

As families were coming in and out of my room,

one of the parents stopped in the middle of the doorframe.

It was awkward

because he was blocking everyone else from entering,

so I went to introduce myself.

"Hi, I'm Mr. Eich," I said, extending my hand. "It's nice to meet you."

His hands stayed at his side,

and instead of shaking hands,

he gave me some history.

"I went to school here, in this very room," he said. "I hated it here . . .

the kids were cruel."

Memories, especially the bad ones,

can really affect how you frame the world.

It's really unfortunate when those negative memories

weren't caused by actions you've taken

but by things that happened *to* you.

I invited the parent to meet me after school later that week,

and I learned all about his past experiences

and the perception he held of the school.

When we were done, he left me with a quote

that has stuck with me.

"I really appreciate you not telling me it will be okay or be

different," he said.

"Thank you for just listening to me."

So that's what I think about

when my students and parents

walk through the doorframe.

Everyone has a story,

and we don't just need to hear them,

we need to listen.

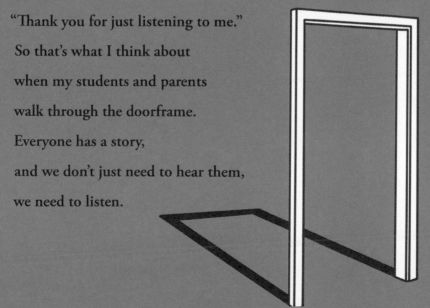

Nail Polish

One of my students, Sophia, had new nail polish or designs
on her nails every Monday.

Every. Monday.

How did I notice? Well, middle schoolers aren't exactly quiet.

"You like my nails, Mr. Eich?!" Sophia said, shoving them to my face.

"Check 'em out!"

"Wow!" I exclaimed. "Those are incredible! How long did it take you?"

Sophia shook her head and laughed.

"I don't do them! My mom does them for me every Monday

because she says there is nothing better

than a boost of confidence to start your week!"

When I look back at this story,

I originally wrote it down because I thought it was cute.

But then I started thinking about how Sophia navigated school,

and she *was* confident.

She did school plays,

volunteered in class,

and took risks in class projects.

So I wonder:

Was she able to do all of that

because that's who she is at her core?

Or was she prepared to do all of that

because her mom took the time

to instill confidence in her daughter,

one painted nail at a time?

Throwing Stars

Two of my students, Devan and Brady, hung out together all the time.

They were the definition of best friends.

In fact, they only hung out together, as far as I could tell.

You would often find them throwing stars at each other.

These folded, origami stars would go flying across the hallway.

"Devan! I got you! That's one point!"

"No, you missed Brady! Take *that*!"

They did this every day . . . every day until Brady's family moved

to another state.

Devan didn't handle it well.

He was distant in class,

refused to eat next to anyone else,

and his grades started slipping too.

I tried my best to help, and we had some good talks,

but I wasn't noticing a change

until one day, something unexpected happened.

We were sitting in class writing in our notebooks when Devan yelled,

"OW! Hey! Who threw this star at me?!"

Mitchell waved from the back of the room.

"Is that one point or two because I hit you in the head?!" he asked. "I

haven't played before."

I froze because I didn't know if this would send Devan over the edge,

but it didn't.

Devan threw it back and hit Mitchell in the shoulder.

"HA! Now we are tied."

Then my classroom turned into a chaotic scene

of shooting stars and laughter between Devan and Mitchell,

and that was okay with me.

We don't always meet new friends formally.

Sometimes it takes a risk from one person,

trust from the other,

and something to hold it all together.

And that day, that something happened to be

a throwing star.

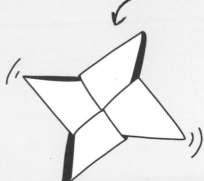

Mop

There are not many things that gross me out about my job.

This is because I have been exposed to the many, many things

kids decide to do

that are absolutely disgusting.

This is one of those stories.

I was in the cafeteria

doing my best to prevent students

from putting mashed potatoes up their noses

or carrots in their friend's ear.

As students were exiting at the end of lunch,

I noticed they were all stepping over something.

A mess, perhaps?

I went and grabbed the mop.

When I got closer to the source,

I got a glimpse of what it was.

It was . . . well, I don't know *what* is was.

But it was brown,

flat,

and goopy.

Before I could get the mop on it,

a student stepped over it,

took two fingers,

scooped up part of the

brown,

flat

goop,

put it in his mouth,

and walked away.

I tell this story to my students

so when they answer a question in class,

I can ask them, "How confident are you?"

Sometimes they will answer,

"As confident as the kid who scooped up the

brown,

flat

goop."

Light Switch

We were taking students up to an environmental learning camp
for the week.

The week before we left, Alan's mom talked to me many times.

"Mr. Eich, I know this is silly, but my son is still afraid of the dark,"
she admitted. "And I really hope his roommates will
be respectful and allow him to have a night-light. . . ."

"Of course!" I assured. "I will make sure he has friends in his room."

Still, she called almost every day before we left.

"Mr. Eich, can he bring his own night-light?"

"Mr. Eich, are their backup night-lights there?"

Alan was about as nervous as his mom too.

"But what if my friends find out I am scared of the dark?!" he
panicked. "They will tease me!"

I could tell this was perhaps going to be a growth opportunity
for both Mom and Alan.

The first night on the trip though, something did go wrong.

We just did our final round to make sure kids were quiet

in their rooms,

when suddenly the power went out.

Kids immediately started laughing and making spooky noises,

and I was laughing for a minute too, until I remembered:

Alan!

I grabbed a flashlight and went to Alan's room,

and when I got there, I saw the most amazing thing.

Alan was on the floor in the center of the room,

but around him were his friends,

a few of them with their hands on his shoulders.

I tell this story to my students often,

because I want them to understand one thing:

you can surround yourself with all kinds of people,

but true friends will surround *you*

when you need them the most.

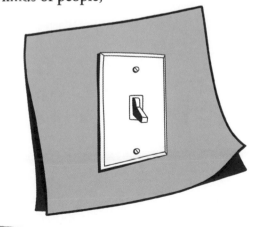

Tapasvi

I had a student named Tapasvi.

She had a warm smile

and a kind heart

and was just a really cool kid to have in the classroom.

I got a call one morning

from her uncle

about five minutes before the day started.

He informed me Tapasvi had been killed

in a horrific car accident.

That was really hard for me to hear

because I was with her every single day.

Every morning to welcome her at the door.

Every afternoon to wave goodbye.

As I processed the news,

the first student of the day walked into my classroom.

His name was Zach.

The first thing out of his mouth was, "What's wrong, Mr. Eich?"

"You usually greet me at the door."

He was so keyed into how we functioned in our relationship

that he already knew something was off.

I don't think everyone understands

the amount of emotional vulnerability

you need to have with kids

when you are teaching.

I don't think they get it.

The amount of time and bonding you do with kids

in a short amount of time

is intense.

That is one reason I write everything down.

I don't want to forget them,

and I will not forget Tapasvi.

Ever.

One Sentence

A parent came into school because we were having a disagreement

on how to navigate their child's education.

It was a very respectful conversation;

we just weren't making any progress in either direction.

I felt my approach was best,

and so did she.

At one point, she stopped the conversation,

and said something I hadn't heard before.

"I want you to know that even though I disagree with you," she began,

"I respect and trust you

because my kid respects and trusts you.

You have my full support to do whatever you think is best.

Just let me know how I can help."

I don't remember this story because I "got my way."

I remember this story

because it is the most respected I've felt in my profession,

and it only took one sentence

to make me feel that way.

I try to measure my own words this way when I speak to others,

especially my students

because I could be one sentence away

from creating a feeling

they haven't felt before.

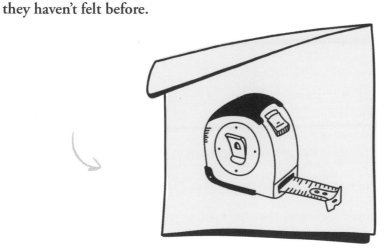

Lunch

I was in the cafeteria watching all five hundred students eat.

Since there are so many kids,

it can be difficult to find one person

at any particular time.

We had a new student from a different country that year named Jirah,

and I wanted to check in with him

to make sure he was adjusting to the chaos

that is the lunchroom.

I couldn't find him.

That happened the next day too.

And the day after that.

So on the third day, I made it a point to find Jirah

and see where he was during lunch.

I ended up finding him in the staff bathroom,

where he had locked himself in a stall.

When he eventually opened the door,

he just sat back on the floor.

"Is everything okay?" I asked. "What is bothering you?"

"I can't watch all the food get thrown away anymore," he said.

"I know people back at home who could use it."

I don't get to travel much,

but the kids I meet from around the world

give me something I hope I never take for granted:

perspective.

Grapes

Everyone was doing some independent reading during literature circles.

In the back of the room, Taisha was not reading.

She was hunched over really engaged in something at her desk.

When I got there, she couldn't contain her excitement.

"Mr. Eich, come here!" she said. "Have you ever noticed the outside of

this grape before?"

"No, I haven't," I said, looking at the grape. "Tell me about it."

"I just discovered it there are all these little rivers running through it,"

she exclaimed. "How have I not discovered this before?"

I let her look at it for the rest of class,

and I read the assignment with her during lunch

so she wouldn't fall behind.

We celebrate when a kid finally gets a concept,

but it's those moments of pure discovery

where you witness such a zest for life,

you just have to wonder what else you may be missing.

So that's what I think about when I see grapes—

what's out there that's been in front of me the entire time,

but I've actually been missing.

Big Elm Tree

I worked with a family who was relentless

in their pursuit of perfection for their child's education.

It was to the point where anything my colleague and I did

wasn't up to the standard they were seeking.

Their child, Amelia, was an absolute delight.

She was kind and bright,

but you could feel the weight of her family

on her shoulders

every day.

Her parents scheduled a lot of meetings with us,

but one particular meeting was different.

We were writing personal narratives in class,

and when Amelia wrote hers, she started crying.

I tried my best to comfort her,

but she didn't want to talk about it.

However,

she let me read her paper.

She wrote that in her backyard was an elm tree,

and she had climbed it since she was little.

It was the one place she felt she had solitude,

but her parents were cutting it down

to make room for a garden.

The way she wrote about her love for that tree

really overwhelmed me.

The parents had Amelia sit in that meeting later that day,

and they told us we needed to do better,

provide more for their daughter,

and push,

push,

push.

It was then I really understood

the importance of that tree

to Amelia.

Witnessing a Risk

My students were writing about a time they realized something.

Naisha came up to me and said, "Only you are going to read this right?"

"Right," I confirmed. "Unless you want to read it to the class?"

She said no, then handed me the paper.

The moment she left, I read it.

It's about her friend Landon

and the moment she realized he was her best friend.

Adorable, right?

But there is more.

I had Landon in my next class and he asked me the same question.

"No one is going to see this right, Mr. Eich?"

"Right," I said.

His narrative was about his neighbor, Naisha,

and the moment he realized what a true friend is.

My heart almost exploded.

Have they said this to each other? Do they know?!

So, I decided to pose them each a question separately.

"That story you wrote is really powerful,

I wonder what would happen

if you showed it to the person you wrote about?"

As a teacher, you watch kids tiptoe to the edge

of what they perceive to be a risk.

I don't think it's my job to reveal the reality of that risk

but rather to get them to think about all the amazing possibilities

that can come from taking it.

In case you are wondering,

Naisha and Landon did show each other those stories,

but not for another two years.

That's a story for another day.

Storm

As a teacher, you don't really know what is walking into

your room each day.

Unpredictable weather, you might say.

This particular day, Luca came into my class,

and he had a look.

Before I could get to him,

he just exploded.

He lost it.

He absolutely lost it.

Screaming

and cussing

and throwing things.

It was a lot all at once.

I was eventually able to calm him down.

I then addressed the situation with the class,

and we moved on with our day.

But the parents of the other students didn't move on

when they heard what happened.

They came to school the next day,

irate that we would let something like this happen in the classroom.

They wanted accountability and consequences,

but they didn't even know Luca.

If they knew him,

they would know he had spent the last three nights

sleeping in a car

in a parking lot.

Sometimes people react with the idea

that if they were in a similar situation,

it would be different.

But the thing about a storm is

we do not always know when it will come

or who is stuck in it.

However, we can still treat everyone

with the love and respect

they deserve

and hopefully

guide them through the storm.

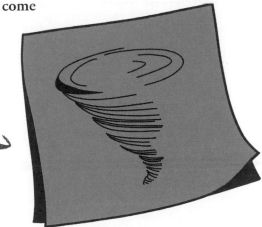

Light

It was my first year teaching, and I had a student named Estrella,

whose name literally translates to "star" in Spanish.

She lived up to the name.

She had a warm presence about her

that drew others in,

and no matter who you were,

Estrella made you feel like you were the center of the room.

One day though,

two students humiliated Estrella

on the bus ride home from school,

and the next day, Estrella's light

was gone.

She was quiet,

reserved,

hesitant.

But that only lasted a day

because the next day, she came back

and was brighter than ever.

She came in and asked the principal

if she could meet with the other students

because she wanted them to know

she forgave them for what they did.

I once heard individuals

are created from the best pieces

learned from other people.

So, from a kid named Estrella,

I learned about light.

Baby Blanket

One of my students, Adrian, was putting all my teacher tools
to the test.

The first day of school, he made a name for himself

by running down the hallway with a Sharpie on the wall,

and his reputation didn't get any better after that.

Incident after incident,

outburst after outburst,

each one was just a major disruption.

But the second week of school,

we asked students to bring in something

they wanted to share with the class

so we could get to know each other better.

When it was Adrian's turn,

he showed the class his baby blanket.

"This is my special blanket," he said. "My mom gave it to me

when I was born,

and I snuggle with it every night, and it reminds

me how much she loves me."

As much as some students (and adults) complicate my day

and sometimes make it difficult,

they are someone's baby.

So, when I am frustrated with someone's behavior,

the baby blanket comes to mind.

The person was at one time a small child,

and no matter who they are or where they come from,

the one thing that a kid needs most from me is the love they deserve,

and I can give that all day.

The Lizard

Students were just arriving for the day,

but I couldn't greet them at the door

because my classroom phone started ringing.

"Good morning! This is Mr. Eich!" I said.

 It went downhill from there.

"This is Lisa, Darren's mom. He took his brother's lizard and put it in

his backpack and . . ."

I could hear shrill screaming from a child in the background of the call.

". . . and please, Mr. Eich, can you get the lizard when he gets to

school, or else he is going to scream like this all day and I—"

The phone call suddenly ended,

and now I had a lizard to find.

As soon as Darren entered the room,

I told him I knew about the lizard.

He immediately panicked and took off running.

It was 7:30 a.m.

It was way too early to be chasing kids

who have kidnapped their brother's lizard.

I located Darren in the bathroom who had his arms wrapped around the backpack.

"Darren," I said calmly. "We need to put the lizard in a container so your mom can pick it up. . . ."

"NO! It's my lizard," He yelled. "Not my brother's!"

"I think you and I can agree we can't have a lizard running around the school, right?"

"But he's mine," Darren argued. "Look!"

Darren opened the backpack, and I got in my most athletic stance, ready to catch a squirming lizard.

"See, Mr. Eich," Darren said. "It has my name on it!"

The "lizard" was a stuffed animal.

There is no lesson here.

I just wanted you to have a glimpse of what it is like to be a teacher.

Erasers

I was teaching sixth grade, and one of my students, André ,

was on a mission.

"I'm starting my own business, Mr. Eich."

"Oh," I said. "What for?"

"Erasers," he said. "Custom-made erasers!"

André told me how he liked to carve names

into the side of those big, pink erasers.

So, he was gonna start selling them:

custom pink erasers.

I watched him set up shop in the hallway

(where all middle school transactions take place),

but opening day was not successful.

Nor was the second,

or any day for that week.

"Why is nobody buying my erasers?!" he said in disgust one afternoon.

"What am I doing wrong?!"

But that next day,

he sold one.

He *actually* sold one.

The second day,

a few more.

By the end of this week,

André had a business.

This is more than a successful small business story though.

André had a passion for custom-made erasers

(which, to be frank, I didn't see a market for).

But he stuck with it

and finally found what most of us are looking for—

an audience.

Cat Pillow

I was at home teaching class online during the height

of the Covid-19 pandemic.

All teachers had to create something called

"Office Hours,"

a single hour dedicated to helping students,

which meant we had to keep our video call open

the entire time.

No one ever showed up

except for Tessa.

She didn't need help with any classwork.

Tessa was there for one thing:

to chat.

I will be honest.

Teaching online was a miserable experience for me.

Any time I could get away from the screen,

I took the chance.

Most days, I hoped Tessa wouldn't show up

so I could have a moment to myself.

But my opinion about that changed one day

when Tessa showed up to my office hours crying.

"Is there anything I can do?" I said,

even though I was on a screen

miles away.

"I'm having a really hard time being home," she said. "Can you

tell me a silly story? My neighbor says you told them to her

class when you were her teacher."

So I told Tessa a story

while she laid on her bed

and snuggled a cat pillow

(a pillow with cats on it).

I've tried my best to analyze this story for a greater lesson.

I've decided it doesn't need to have one.

It's just something I want to remember,

and I wanted to share it with you.

Snail

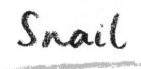

We were celebrating the end of our writing unit.

To do this, students were making clay sculptures

of where their story took place.

They had five days to complete them in class.

Daniella was on pace to finish in five years.

To be fair, she wasn't distracted

or causing problems.

She was diligent.

Careful.

"My mom says I am a snail," Daniella told me. "She tells me to hurry

up a lot."

"Oh, really?" I said, "How do you feel about that?"

"I dunno," Daniella shrugged. "I guess I just like going at the speed

I'm going."

Daniella finally finished one day.

It didn't take her five years to complete it,

but it felt that way.

If you compared her sculpture to the rest,

it didn't stand out one way or another.

But since I got to watch her make it,

I viewed it much differently than the others.

We live in a time where everything is fast.

Fast food.

Fast delivery.

Faster internet speeds.

I think we start to believe everything we do should be done

at the same pace.

There may be deadlines

or things you need to get done,

but I am starting to think the best approaches

aren't necessarily the fast ones

or the slow ones

but the ones that feel just right.

Key Chains

It was "Surprise Me!" week in class,

a week I invented to help students get to know each other.

Each student got to bring something in

to show or tell

that would "surprise" the class with information

they didn't know about the individual.

I know this sounds like show-and-tell,

and it is,

but I like my name better.

Anyway, Sasha decided to bring in part of her key chain collection.

I didn't write down how many she had.

I just remember thinking

if this is only "part" of the collection,

how does she have room at home

for the rest of them?

"Each of these represents a place I've been," she explained.

"So how many do you want to collect?" a classmate blurted.

Sasha paused for a second, her eyes looking up.

"I don't want to collect key chains, actually," she said. "I just want to experience the place."

Memories are kind of like key chains, aren't they?

I'm sure this comparison has been made before,

but I wonder how many of us have forgotten

to truly live the experience

rather than just collecting them.

Grandpa Joe

On Mondays, I like to make a point of asking students

to share something from the weekend.

It's a way to get to know them better

and ease into our week.

Some students share very little,

but those who love the spotlight

tend to share everything.

Jada was one of those people.

Most Mondays, she talked about her Grandpa Joe.

"We went swimming in the pond behind his house," Jada said. "We saw

three dragonflies!"

And another time. . . .

"Grandpa Joe took me out for breakfast and let me have *three* donuts!"

It was always a Grandpa Joe story,

no matter what.

One day, I called Jada's parents

to let them know she had a missing assignment.

I also mentioned how much we enjoyed listening to Jada
retell her weekend adventures with Grandpa Joe.
As it turns out,
Grandpa Joe had passed away last summer.
Jada's mom had no idea she talked about him
as if he were still here.
I once heard you can't tell anyone how to grieve
because until you go through it,
you won't understand the emotional toll it takes
just to get out of bed some days.
I do not know where Jada's grandpa is right now.
But I like to imagine that wherever he is,
he is retelling the same stories
of his adventures with Jada.

The Basket Maker

Our school hosted a group of professionals from various careers

so our students could be exposed to all sorts of different jobs.

This is typically known as "Career Day."

It's also a great day for me

because I am not in charge of the event,

so I get to walk around,

see what students choose,

and learn more about them.

One of the volunteers for the program

was a professional basket maker.

I know what you are thinking.

I didn't know they existed either.

One of my students, Ilhan, was in the front row asking a lot

of questions.

He was very polite,

and his questions were all on topic too,

which was impressive for a middle schooler.

However, the volunteer was getting annoyed with his questions

and became very dismissive toward Ilhan.

He did not take this well,

and he suddenly became very defensive.

"Why are you ignoring me?!" he asked.

"Because you are asking too many questions," she said abruptly.

"I am here to tell you what I do, not how I do it."

To which Ilhan responded,

"But what's wrong with wanting to know more?"

Nothing.

The answer should always be that.

Nothing.

Megaphone

When one of my colleagues retired, she gifted me a megaphone

she kept in her classroom.

I was thrilled!

Having a megaphone when you are outside

with hundreds of children is a game changer,

so I was looking forward to my new,

powerful,

outside voice.

The first day of recess, one of my students, Giana,

asked if she could carry it outside for me.

Giana was, for lack of a better term,

intimidatingly awesome.

She was strong but gentle.

Smart but not arrogant.

Persistent but not overbearing.

And she treated everyone in a way that made them feel special.

Still, I was reluctant to let her carry it

because I didn't want something to happen to my new,

powerful,

outside voice.

But I let her anyway

because she said she would be "super careful."

When I got outside with the rest of class,

I saw the megaphone on the concrete,

and it was broken into pieces.

"I dropped it, Mr. Eich," she said, already tearing up. "I am so, so sorry."

I was too, because my new,

powerful,

outside voice

was gone.

At the end of recess, I tried yelling to get everyone's attention.

It didn't work.

That's when Giana stepped up on the picnic table and powerfully yelled,

"Recess is over *right now*!"

Everyone stopped what they were doing immediately and went inside,

not because they were scared of her.

But because that's what happens

when you are respected.

———

The Line

It was the last day of school,

and we had a pizza party picnic lunch to celebrate.

When the pizza arrived, all of our students ran to get in line

so they could secure the best possible pizza slice.

There was a lot of jockeying for positions,

but eventually a line formed.

However, the line continued to change

as some students asked to stand next to friends

or move up in line because they were "really hungry."

One student, Ciara, kept shifting closer

and closer

to the back of the line.

She was gracious though, saying things like,

"You can budge me so you can be with your friend,"

or

"I'm hungry too, but you can budge me if you want."

Eventually, Ciara found herself at the very end of the line.

When she finally got to the table,

the pizza was gone.

I assured her I would get more, but she brushed it off.

"It's okay, Mr. Eich," she said. "I can wait to eat until I get home."

A few minutes later, a delivery car rolled up

because they had left one pizza in the car by accident,

so I gave the entire pizza to Ciara,

and instead of two slices,

she had many more.

It doesn't always turn out that way for people like Ciara.

I wish it did more often.

Because those are the people

whose kindness

and patience

hold the world together.

Stardust

My fifth year teaching

was one of my most memorable groups of students

for a variety of reasons.

One trait that stood out right away

was they all got along with one another.

Seriously.

I could pair a kid with any other,

make a group of any size,

and it would be a success.

A teacher's dream!

Two months into the school year, a new student was added to

my class:

Ezekial.

Upon arrival, it was clear he had significant delays

in both cognitive functioning

and fine motor skills.

He would have conversations with himself,

chew his hands,

and blurt out long, unrecognizable sounds.

Our school received no information when he enrolled,

so we were not prepared.

But somehow, my students were.

During Ezekial's third day of school, he arrived late to class

and announced his entrance by yelling

"Stardust!"

at the top of his lungs.

For reasons I cannot explain,

my entire class yelled back in unison

"Stardust!"

And for the first time since we met,

Ezekial smiled.

We are all so different in so many ways,

but that doesn't mean we can't discover new ways

to find each other.

Apple

It was the second week of school, and my students wanted to
celebrate my birthday.

"Let's have a pizza party and bring in balloons and get a cake!"
they begged.

"That's kind of you all," I said. "But you don't need to buy me
anything. We'll just play a fun game."

But that didn't stop some of them.

The day of my birthday, some students brought in some gifts.

I got some homemade cookies,

a few gift cards,

and some hand-drawn pictures.

And then we went to lunch, where the real story begins.

While I was walking around the cafeteria,

I noticed Blaine put an apple in his pocket.

This isn't strange at all when you consider what else happens
in a cafeteria on a daily basis.

Blaine beat me back to class.

I knew because when I arrived,

there was an apple on my desk with a note.

"Sorry I didn't get you anything special, Mr. Eich. I know you like

apples, so I got you this."

I understand that gift-giving is a specific love language,

but not all kids understand that,

so you have to remind them

what is most important.

"Hey, Blaine, I really appreciate how you thought to get me some-

thing," I said. "But you need to know *you* being in *this* classroom

is pretty special,

so you know what I really want for my birthday?"

"No. . . ." he said, confused.

"Would you be on my team for our next game? That would be a

great birthday gift."

An apple, to me, represents so much more

than the stereotypical teacher gift.

It's about connecting with people.

It always has been,

and it always will be.

Vacuum

If you have never experienced being a teacher, then you might

not know the pain, the *agony*,

of having to repeat directions over and over and over again.

I tell them what to do.

I put it on the board.

I put it on their papers

(in large, bold font),

and I repeat *where* to find these directions too.

I have to give directions

and then more directions

on where to find directions.

Think about *that* for a few minutes,

and you might experience the headache of a teacher.

I do not blame students for their inability to remember

all the places where I have put directions.

I know their brains have a lot going on.

So that is why Santiago's actions stood out

in the chaos of everyone asking me for directions.

"Hey, Mr. Eich, I made a mess in the back of the room by accident,"

he said. "Do you have a vacuum I could use to clean it up?"

Our minds are usually preoccupied with *something*,

even if we don't recognize it is.

We have conversations while thinking of something else,

and we complete tasks while simultaneously doing others.

So when someone like Santiago

jumps outside all that disorder

and remembers to do something like clean up a mess

without being told,

without directions,

it makes me feel like everything is going to be okay.

I know that seems silly,

but when you see how forgetful people can be sometimes,

it gives me a sense of hope

I cannot explain.

Arboretum

We went on a field trip to the Minnesota Landscape Arboretum

so students could learn about agriculture and urban gardening.

One of my students, Ra'King, was completely captivated

by every piece of information,

but especially anything that mentioned

trees.

Luckily for Ra'King,

there is a three-mile drive around the property

where you can park

and walk

among many different species of trees.

It was hard to keep Ra'King to stay with the group

because he kept running ahead

to be the first one

to touch every tree.

"Mr. Eich! Look at *this* one!" he said. "I can't get my arms around it!"

Our instructor then pointed out that new trees

are currently being invented and grown

by the University of Minnesota.

That was news to me.

And, of course, Ra'King.

"What?! That is awesome!" he exclaimed. "I'm going to invent a new tree

someday too!"

"I doubt it," a friend teased. "Why do you think you can?"

"Somebody is going to do it," he shot back. "So why not me?!"

We often find ourselves stuck at the beginning of a dream

because we believe there are others who will do it better

or do it first.

But regardless,

somebody *is* going to do it . . .

so, it might as well be you.

Poop

We had just got back in the classroom after lunch when I smelled it.

Unfortunately, this was not the first time I would need to track down

the source of a bad smell.

It happens *often* in the classroom.

Discretely trying to smell thirty different kids

is not the easiest thing to do either.

You don't want to bring attention to someone,

but you also don't want to sit in the smell

any longer than you have to.

There was a kid sitting on a giant yoga ball, gently bouncing on it.

Could it be him?

There was another student who kept adjusting her pants.

Could it be her?

Everyone is a suspect.

I did a few rounds around the room,

doing my best to avoid getting caught

while smelling each area.

A few students were beginning to notice the smell too,

which added unwanted pressure

to an already tense-filled situation.

"Do you smell that?" one kid said. "It smells like a nasty."

"Yeah," agreed another student. "It's getting worse."

By the end of class, I had not discovered the source,

but as they left, one student, Emilee, stayed behind

and asked to speak with me.

"Mr. Eich, you smell like poop," she said politely. "I thought you

should know."

I did a quick glance around my body,

even though I was confident she was wrong.

But there *it* was.

Stuck on the bottom of my shoe.

When we have a problem or conflict,

we tend to look at others to blame,

when in reality,

maybe the first place we need to look

is at ourselves.

Go-Karts

Students were working on an engineering challenge

where they needed to design a self-propelled miniature go-kart.

Typically, there are three approaches to the design of the kart:

use of rubber bands,

use of a ramp,

or use of air (balloons).

We provide all the materials to complete any of these three designs,

including instructions for the base model.

The challenge lies in the redesign.

The go-kart designs will only go so far,

so students have to figure out another way

for the karts to go *farther*.

Retesting the kart as you redesign will also test your patience.

So when you are working with a partner,

that test of patience is magnified.

Can you feel the tension already?

Many students need at least one quick counseling session

to work through their frustrations about their partners.

Brooke and Imani were headed in that direction.

They were not friends.

They were not enemies though either.

They were just two kids who happened to be in a group together,

and they each had their own idea of what to do.

Eventually, they reached a compromise—

a go-kart with a balloon attached to each wheel.

It was clunky and wobbly, but it managed to move forward

ever so slightly.

Compromise is not easy

because we feel like we are giving up part of ourselves.

But we can't forget progress is still progress.

It may be clunky, it may be wobbly,

but it is still moving forward

ever so slightly.

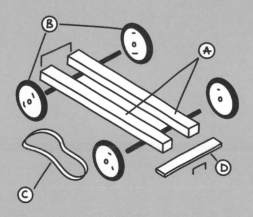

Spoon

We were doing a fundraiser for our school, and teachers were asked

to come up with class goals and celebration incentives to help

motivate students and families.

My students couldn't decide on a single thing.

Pizza party?

No.

Extra recess?

Not good enough.

Pie the teacher in the face?

Boring.

As a joke, I told the class I could do a blind taste test.

I have never seen children agree on something so quickly in my

entire life.

"Okay, I'll do it," I agreed, "but you have to raise *this* much money."

It was a large amount they would never hit,

which was purposefully chosen

because I did not want to do a blind taste test.

They reached the goal in less than forty-eight hours.

A month later, I sat in a chair with a blindfold on,

mentally preparing to eat thirty different things

with no idea what any of them were.

There were only three rules:

whatever I ate couldn't be alive,

it had to be food,

and it had to fit on a single spoon.

"I've been waiting for this moment all month," a student whispered

in my ear

as they pressed a spoon up to my lips.

I took my first bite of thirty different things,

from thirty different middle school students.

And if that isn't an example of trust,

then I don't know what is.

Pushpins

Carlos was the clumsiest student I had ever met.

He would bump into corners,

drop his materials,

and break things by accident

almost every day.

It happened so often,

I began to wonder if it was an act

because believe it or not,

some kids will humiliate themselves

in order to get attention.

But Carlos was not like that.

He was just clumsy.

The clumsiest of all.

One day, while Carlos was walking around the room he tripped

and bumped into my desk.

My coffee spilled,

paper stacks fell over,

and my jar of pushpins

went crashing to the ground.

"He did it *again*!" a student blurted out. "Carlos, you are always bumping

into things!"

As Carlos helped me pick up all the pushpins off the carpet,

he said, "Do you think I will always be like this, Mr. Eich?"

Changing your reputation is never easy.

Besides convincing others you are different,

you have to convince someone else first:

you have to convince *yourself.*

"Your opinion is the most important," I said. "What do you think?"

Carlos dropped the last pushpin into the glass jar.

"No, I will not," he said with confidence. "I am not clumsy."

And you know what?

I believe him.

Ping-Pong

The best purchases I ever made as a teacher were portable ping-pong sets.

You could quickly set it up on any table and transform the classroom

into a sporting event,

and middle school students are always in need of a quick brain break.

One day, we finished our lesson early,

so I brought out the portable ping-pong set.

The competitive students quickly made a tournament bracket

because they all wanted to play the best student in class:

Edward.

Edward was not just good—he was incredible.

A two-time Junior Olympic qualifier,

he could easily beat kids without moving his feet.

But he had one problem: he was extremely cocky.

A crowd quickly formed to watch Edward quickly dispatch his opponents

as he teased and trash-talked them,

but one student, Mya, watched from farther away.

Her eyes followed the ball back and forth,

back and forth,

as Edward tore through the competition.

It didn't take long for Edward to beat everyone,

but as students moved to other tables to play each other,

one student stepped forward to face Edward.

It was Mya.

Mya served the ball awkwardly, and it hit the net.

She tried again. It hit the net.

Mya put the paddle down and began to walk away.

"Have you . . . played before?" Edward asked.

"No," Mya said hesitantly. "Can you teach me?"

"No one has ever asked me that," Edward paused.

By the end of class, Mya and Edward were hitting the ball
back and forth.

Edward was teaching Mya how to hit the ball;

Mya was teaching Edward how to be gentle.

That's a pretty cool back-and-forth.

The Tick

I was in the middle of teaching when a scream came

from the back of the room.

"AGH!" Zahara yelled. "There is a tick on my arm!"

Whether or not the rest of the class was scared of ticks didn't matter.

They all proceeded to scream, then ran away from Zahara

all the way to the front of the room.

I went over to Zahara to investigate.

"Where is it?" I asked. "Where did it go?"

"I'm not sure," she said, looking at the floor. "I flicked it off."

"I am *not* going back to my seat until we find it," declared another

student.

"Me either," said another. "Not until I know it's gone."

"We will *never* find it though," another blurted. "But we could try?"

Others nodded their heads in agreement.

Thus began the start of a seemingly impossible mission:

thirty middle school students and their teacher

attempting to find a single brown tick

on the dark blue carpet of a classroom floor.

I had zero faith we would find it.

I had zero faith we would go back to the lesson.

Still, on our hands and knees, all of us searched.

Which, in hindsight, was probably ideal for the tick

to find his next host.

In any case, we persisted.

We searched, we hunted,

but we never found the tick.

You know what, though?

Even though the odds were stacked against us,

and the probability of success was slim,

we still decided to try,

and that is something we can all be proud of.

Juice Box

There were two girls in my homeroom, Kingsley and Zoey,

who came up with the strangest competitions.

I wish I could tell you about all of them

but that would require its own separate book, but here is one:

"Juice Box Shot."

The game is straightforward.

One person holds a juice box with the straw inserted facing the partner.

The person holding the juice box then squeezes slightly,

which shoots a stream of liquid toward the partner.

The partner then attempts to catch the liquid in their mouth.

Laughter ensues.

I didn't understand the game the first time I saw it.

It seemed more like an excuse to make a purposeful mess

rather than play a game.

"How did you invent *this* one?" I asked one day.

"We didn't," Zoey said while taking a juice box from her backpack.

"It happened by accident."

"A happy accident," chimed Kingsley.

Zoey proceeded to tell me that earlier in the month,

Kingsley and Zoey had gotten into an argument in the cafeteria.

The argument was over something "stupid," she said,

but they were both very angry with each other.

"I just squeezed my juice box because I was so upset," Kingsley said,

"and some of it shot out and went in Zoey's mouth!"

"It was over something *so* stupid," said Zoey.

"Sooooo, soooooo stupid," Kingsley agreed.

"And now you just play this game?" I asked.

"It reminds us not to argue over silly things," they said together laughing.

So that's what I think about when I see a juice box.

Am I arguing over something I truly care about,

or is soooooo, soooooo stupid?

Flashlight

By the time students reach middle school, most of them are

past the point of imaginary things.

I won't list them here, in case a kid is reading this book,

but hopefully you understand what I mean.

Occasionally though, there will be a child who believes

in something so passionately,

you begin to question if it's real or not.

For Ferris, it happened to be monsters.

When I say "monster,"

I am not referring to bigfoot,

the Loch Ness Monster,

or the abominable snowman.

For all I know, they could be real.

I am referring to the monsters Ferris says live under his bed

and in his closet.

I believe those to be fake, and I think most people would agree.

But not Ferris.

To him, they are *very* real, and pose a *real* threat

every night he climbs into bed.

He has shared this belief in class multiple times.

Shared it with kids who do not believe in monsters

and who go to bed without fear of being eaten.

Unlike Ferris,

who thinks he is first on the menu

every single night.

The other students disagreed,

but they never argued or dismissed his idea.

They just supported him in his journey

offering advice, suggestions,

and one time even a flashlight,

which he promptly accepted.

I do not believe in monsters,

but I do think that helping others,

no matter what we believe,

is a key way

to connect with each other.

Winter Gloves

One of my students, Anton, told me he was going to have something really cool

to show me the next day.

"You're gonna love it, Mr. Eich. I just know it."

When a middle schooler says that phrase,

you never know what you're gonna get.

When he arrived the next day, I was pretty curious

about what would be revealed.

It turned out to be something I would have never guessed.

"Do you like them, Mr. Eich?" Anton asked excitedly. "What do

you think?"

Anton was holding up his hands,

which had winter gloves on them.

The gloves were clearly old and worn.

The leather was cracking at the top,

and between the thumb and the fingers were dark, worn lines

from some sort of repetitive work.

"These were my grandpa's," he said. "I asked if I could have them, and he said yes!"

"That's awesome, Anton," I said. "But I am curious, why would you want a used pair?"

"I just think they are the coolest," Anton said, and then he went off to join his friends.

At first, I thought it was just that.

The gloves looked cool,

and so Anton was happy to get them.

A classic "I want it, I got it" story from a middle schooler.

But I have a feeling the gloves weren't wanted

because of the way they looked.

As we grow, even as adults, I think we are always looking

for someone to emulate.

Sometimes we can't verbalize what exactly we want to be.

Maybe it's a feeling, a desire to be someone you look up to.

For Anton, I am guessing that person was his grandpa.

It wasn't the gloves that were special,

but the idea they brought Anton one step closer

to becoming the person he wanted to be like.

Paper Airplane

I was writing on the board when I was suddenly struck

in the back of the head.

It didn't hurt at all, but it definitely got my attention.

I looked at the floor to see what it was:

a paper airplane.

A classic middle school antic.

When I turned around to face the class, I didn't have to ask who did it

because Bruno's eyes were open so wide,

I could see the guilt in his soul.

"I really didn't mean to!" Bruno suddenly blurted. "It was an accident!"

A flashback to when I was in fourth grade:

I threw a paper airplane in class, and it landed on my teacher's lap

as he was reading a book.

Unlike Bruno, I did not apologize

and instead waited in my seat for my punishment.

That is not what happened.

Instead, my teacher asked me a question,

"Did it fly straight or did it turn?"

I was baffled.

"It turned," I said.

He handed me my paper airplane.

"Then I guess I better show you how to make it go straight

so it doesn't end up in my lap again."

So, he taught me what I needed to know.

I went over to Bruno's desk and asked him a question.

"Did it fly straight or did it turn?"

"It curved," he said cautiously.

"Well then, I guess we need to figure out how to make it go straight,"

I said.

"I'll teach you."

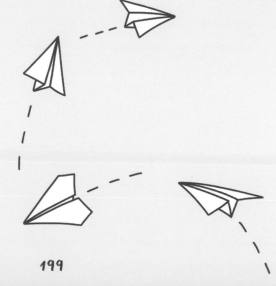

Acknowledgments

Thank you to my wife, Briana:
From the first word of my first project, you believed in me.
Your love, encouragement, and support
continues to fill my creative spirit.

My extraordinary literary agent, Dani:
What started as a call for advice has turned into an opportunity
I sought after for so long:
A chance to tell stories.
I am so thankful for your guidance, persistence, and friendship
as we continue on this adventure together.

My editor, Jean:
For seeing the potential of these stories
and helping bring them to life.

Andrews McMeel Publishing:
For giving me the opportunity to live out a dream.

About the Author

Matt Eicheldinger is a middle school teacher, author, public speaker, and storyteller. His stories on social media have amassed more than 70 million views as he takes viewers through hundreds of memories he has collected over the years, many of which are from his teaching career. He is also the author of many middle-grade novels, including *Matt Sprouts and the Curse of the Ten Broken Toes* and *Matt Sprouts and the Day Nora Ate the Sun.*

You can learn more about Eicheldinger by visiting www.matteicheldinger.com or hear more stories on his Instagram @matteicheldinger.

Andrews McMeel Publishing
a division of Andrews McMeel Universal
1130 Walnut Street, Kansas City, Missouri 64106
www.andrewsmcmeel.com

24 25 26 27 28 RLP 10 9 8 7 6 5 4 3 2 1

ISBN: 978-1-5248-9435-1

Library of Congress Control Number: 2024934986

Editor: Jean Z. Lucas
Art Director: Tiffany Meairs
Designer: Adrian Morgan
Illustrations: Matthew Eicheldinger
Production Editor: Jasmine Lim
Production Manager: Tamara Haus

ATTENTION: SCHOOLS AND BUSINESSES
Andrews McMeel books are available at quantity discounts with bulk
purchase for educational, business, or sales promotional use. For information,
please e-mail the Andrews McMeel Publishing Special Sales Department:
sales@amuniversal.com.